Islamization and Archaeology

DEBATES IN ARCHAEOLOGY
Series editor: Richard Hodges

Against Cultural Property, John Carman
The Anthropology of Hunter-Gatherers, Vicki Cummings
Archaeologies of Conflict, John Carman
Archaeology, Timothy Insoll
Archaeology and International Development in Africa, Colin Breen and Daniel Rhodes
Archaeology and State Theory, Bruce Routledge
Archaeology and Text, John Moreland
Archaeology and the Pan-European Romanesque, Tadhg O'Keeffe
Beyond Celts, Germans and Scythians, Peter S. Wells
Bronze Age Textiles, Klavs Randsborg
Building Colonialism, Daniel T. Rhodes
The Byzantine Dark Ages, Michael J. Decker
Changing Natures, Bill Finlayson and Graeme M. Warren
Combat Archaeology, John Schofield
Debating the Archaeological Heritage, Robin Skeates
Early European Castles, Oliver Creighton
Early Islamic North Africa, Corisande Fenwick
Early Islamic Syria, Alan Walmsley
Empowering Communities through Archaeology and Heritage, Peter G. Gould
Ethics and Burial Archaeology, Duncan Sayer
Evidential Reasoning in Archaeology, Robert Chapman and Alison Wylie
Fishing and Shipwreck Heritage, Sean A. Kingsley
Fluid Pasts, Matthew Edgeworth
From Stonehenge to Mycenae, John C. Barrett and Michael J. Boyd
Gerasa and the Decapolis, David Kennedy

Heritage, Communities and Archaeology, Laurajane Smith and Emma Waterton
Houses and Society in the Later Roman Empire, Kim Bowes
Image and Response in Early Europe, Peter S. Wells
Indo-Roman Trade, Roberta Tomber
Loot, Legitimacy and Ownership, Colin Renfrew
Lost Civilization, James L. Boone
Museums and the Construction of Disciplines, Christopher Whitehead
The Origins of the Civilization of Angkor, Charles F. W. Higham
The Origins of the English, Catherine Hills
Pagan and Christian, David Petts
The Remembered Land, Jim Leary
Rethinking Wetland Archaeology, Robert Van de Noort and Aidan O'Sullivan
The Roman Countryside, Stephen L. Dyson
Roman Reflections, Klavs Randsborg
Shaky Ground, Elizabeth Marlowe
Shipwreck Archaeology of the Holy Land, Sean A. Kingsley
Social Evolution, Mark Pluciennik
State Formation in Early China, Li Liu and Xingcan Chen
The State in Ancient Egypt, Juan Carlos Moreno Garcia
Towns and Trade in the Age of Charlemagne, Richard Hodges
Tradition and Transformation in Anglo-Saxon England, Susan Oosthuizen
Vessels of Influence, Nicole Coolidge Rousmaniere
Villa to Village, Riccardo Francovich and Richard Hodges

Islamization and Archaeology

Religion, Culture and New Materialism

José C. Carvajal López

BLOOMSBURY ACADEMIC
LONDON • NEW YORK • OXFORD • NEW DELHI • SYDNEY

BLOOMSBURY ACADEMIC
Bloomsbury Publishing Plc
50 Bedford Square, London, WC1B 3DP, UK
1385 Broadway, New York, NY 10018, USA
29 Earlsfort Terrace, Dublin 2, Ireland

BLOOMSBURY, BLOOMSBURY ACADEMIC and the Diana logo are trademarks
of Bloomsbury Publishing Plc

First published in Great Britain 2023
Paperback edition published 2025

Copyright © José C. Carvajal López, 2023

José C. Carvajal López has asserted his right under the Copyright, Designs and
Patents Act, 1988, to be identified as Author of this work.

For legal purposes the Acknowledgements on p. xi constitute an extension of
this copyright page.

Cover design: Terry Woodley
Cover image © PEDRE/Getty

All rights reserved. No part of this publication may be reproduced or transmitted
in any form or by any means, electronic or mechanical, including photocopying,
recording, or any information storage or retrieval system, without prior
permission in writing from the publishers.

Bloomsbury Publishing Plc does not have any control over, or responsibility for,
any third-party websites referred to or in this book. All internet addresses given
in this book were correct at the time of going to press. The author and publisher
regret any inconvenience caused if addresses have changed or sites have ceased
to exist, but can accept no responsibility for any such changes.

A catalogue record for this book is available from the British Library.

Library of Congress Cataloging-in-Publication Data
Names: Carvajal López, José Cristóbal, 1979- author.
Title: Islamization and archaeology : religion, culture and new
materialism / José C. Carvajal López.
Description: New York : Bloomsbury Academic, 2023. | Series: Debates in
archaeology | Includes bibliographical references and index.
Identifiers: LCCN 2022049403 | ISBN 9781350006669 (hardback) | ISBN
9781350231597 (paperback) | ISBN 9781350006676 (epub) | ISBN
9781350006683 (ebook)
Subjects: LCSH: Islamic civilization. | Islamic antiquities. | Material culture—
Islamic Empire. | Islamic Empire—Intellectual life.
Classification: LCC DS36.85 .C37 2023 | DDC 909/.09767—dc23/eng/20221115
LC record available at https://lccn.loc.gov/2022049403

ISBN:	HB:	978-1-3500-0666-9
	PB:	978-1-3502-3159-7
	ePDF:	978-1-3500-0668-3
	eBook:	978-1-3500-0667-6

Series: Debates in Archaeology

Typeset by RefineCatch Limited, Bungay, Suffolk

To find out more about our authors and books visit www.bloomsbury.com
and sign up for our newsletters.

To Julio and Emma.

To my colleagues and students at the Department of Archaeology of the University of Sheffield and UCL Qatar.

Contents

List of Figures and Tables	x
Acknowledgements	xi

1	Introduction: Islam and Islamization	1
2	Islamization: From Conversion to Cultural Change	21
3	Islamic Identity and *Being Islamic*	45
4	Islamic Things, Islamic Beings and Con-Text	69
5	Islamization of Communities: Two Case Studies in Early Islam	93
6	Conclusion	133

Notes	143
Bibliography	151
Index	173

Figures and Tables

Figures

4.1 Al-Aqṣā Mosque between 1940 and 1946 (Matson Collection, Library of Congress of the USA, Public Domain)   74

4.2 Bowl 21/1965 of the David Collection. Image by Pernille Klemp. Courtesy of the David Collection, Copenhagen   74

5.1 Map of the Vega of Granada, showing the towns in the region in the early Islamic period. Map elaborated by Jorge Rouco Collazo   96

5.2 Ceramic types from the Vega of Granada discussed in this chapter. The scale is indicative, as sizes are variable within a range. Elaborated by the author   103

5.3 Map of the Gulf with indication of the sites discussed in the text. Map elaborated by Jorge Rouco Collazo   116

5.4 A set of net weights found in Yughbī and abandoned in Phase I (*c.* 674–778 CE). The disposition of the items is as ascertained from their *in situ* position. Picture from the Crowded Desert Project   126

Tables

5.1 Table showing the phases of development of the Islamization of the Vega of Granada   98

5.2 Data about the net weights retrieved Phase II of Yughbī. Key: Wgt = Weight in g; Th = Average thickness in cm; Wdt = Maximum width in cm; Lgt = Maximum length in cm. Data from the Crowded Desert Project   127

Acknowledgements

This book was first conceived in 2015 as something quite different. After more than a decade looking into Islamization, I wanted to discuss my thoughts from the perspective of its impact in identities, in communities and in technologies. In fact, those words were present in the very title of the work at the beginning. But life had other plans. A set of rather complicated changes in my professional life, a long and unexpected illness, a global pandemic and a divorce got in the way. The book that I had initially expected to write in one year took me a more than seven years. There is no sorrow in here, however. The duration of the journey has changed my work completely and its title, and has made it so much more worthwhile. It also means that there are many people I need to thank for their unfailing support.

My first words of acknowledgement are to Richard Hodges, my mentor and friend for so long. He was the person who suggested I write about Islamization for Bloomsbury, one of the many times that he has supported me professionally and personally through my career. My editors at Bloomsbury – Alice Wright, Lily Mac Mahon and Georgina Leighton – are a team of wonderful professionals who endured my delays with patience, and who only had words of encouragement during all the difficult times that I had while composing the manuscript. Finally, the anonymous peer reviewer made insightful and useful comments that helped to improve the text. The reader should know that this book would have not been possible without any of them.

I have been extremely fortunate during my career to be able to learn from the work, example and discussions of many admirable colleagues and students in the fields that this book touches upon (Islamic archaeology, archaeological theory and, to a smaller extent, the archaeology of materials and of Arabia). I trust that the bibliography will reflect the extent of my intellectual debt to some of them, but there are many others beyond. I certainly would not be the archaeologist that

I am today if it were not for my colleagues in several communities of which I am or I have been part. My acknowledgement goes to former and present members of the Research Group *Toponimia, Historia y Arqueología del Reino de Granada* (University of Granada), the Butrint Foundation, the board members of the Journal of Islamic Archaeology, the International Association for the Study of Arabia, the Seminar for Arabian Studies, the members of *The Crowded Desert Project*, the members of the project *Materiality and Preservation in Islamic Contexts* and the Ḥajar Group. Above all, however, I would like to place the three communities that have contributed more to shaping this book in particular: the Department of Archaeology of the University of Sheffield, UCL Qatar and the School of Archaeology and Ancient History of the University of Leicester. In particular, I would like to dedicate this book to Sheffield, under threat of closure, and Qatar, closed since the end of 2020. The sad end of these communities of scholarship is proof of the narrow-mindedness of the current leadership of higher education in the UK. I hope that this book demonstrates the value of supporting and fostering communities like these in the future.

Beyond these communities, I would like to acknowledge the friendship and support of those whose advice and/or example has helped me to shape my ideas about Islamization (although they do not necessarily endorse them!). I must mention here Ibrahim Abu Aemar, Robert Carter, Maribel Fierro, Guillermo García-Contreras Cortés, Marcos García García, Alejandro García Sanjuán, Alexandrine Guérin, Sarah Inskip, Tim Insoll, Ibrahim Abu Iremeis, Miguel Jiménez Puertas, Derek Kennet, Eneko López Martínez de Marigorta, Stephen MacPhillips, José María Martín Civantos, Faisal Al-Naʿīmī, Hagit Nol, Gaetano Palumbo, Andrew Petersen, Tim Power, Seth Priestman, Elena Salinas Pleguezuelo, Irina Shingiray, Jorge de Torres Rodríguez, Joanita Vroom and Bethany Walker. My students in UCL Qatar, coming from all over the world, showed me how important it was to find a way to understand Islam and Islamization that was at the same time respectful of Islamic people but also understandable beyond the Western mindset. I have also been blessed with the insight of two extremely bright doctoral students that I had the pleasure of supervising. They have an interest in Islamization from very different perspectives: thank you, Jelena Živković and Mikel Herrán Subiñas for teaching me so much.

I owe the theoretical approach of this book to my interactions with the thriving Material Worlds Research Centre at the University of Leicester. It is impossible to overstate the thrill that I felt when I found out that New Materialist theories were so useful in helping to explain Islamization for archaeologists. The conversations that I had with members of this community were enriching, but it was, above all, Oliver Harris and Rachel Crellin who guided my exploration of this promising field with steady hands. Ollie, in particular, who was always ready to hold long conversations and endless banter about Deleuze (hardly surprising to anyone who knows him), made this part of the journey particularly enjoyable.

Finally, the love and friendship of many people was crucial in giving me the strength to continue writing through difficult times. Some of those people did not end the journey with me, but I want to acknowledge the time that they gave me. Of those who are still here, I want to mention the names of José Miguel Aguilera Ramiro and Elena Bandos Marsheva, Natalia Álvarez Sanchez, Belén Barrera Aranda, Maite Belloso Sánchez and Antonio Muñoz Frías, Teresa Bonet García and Rocco Corselli, Radha Dalal, Peter Day and Lena Papapanagiotu, David Edwards, Fernando Fernández Iglesias, Alejandro Gámez Arroyo and Macarena Ballesteros Carrasco, Carmen Gámez Arroyo, Axel García Chacón, Samantha Garwood and Jacob Nickels, Myrto Georgakopoulou and Tom Loughlin, Mario Gutiérrez Jiménez, Simon and Jill James, Ying Liu, Andy Merrills and Julia Farley, Anna Mkhitaryan, Enrique Molina Milla, Rubén Montoya, Nataly Papadopoulou, Julio Román Punzón and Maribel Mancilla Cabello, Deirdre O'Sullivan, Odile Rouard, Jorge Rouco Collazo and Cristina Martínez Carrillo, Alice Samson, Sandro Sebastiani, Veronica Testolini and Will Severs, Lenore Thompson and Liam Lee, Christina Tsoraki and Ben Chan, Beatricce Vacca, Ruth Young and all the members of the Leicester Outdoors Fitness group, but especially Tony Dandy and Bonita Robinson, Huw Barton and Phoebe MacDonald, Joe Christy, Lina Gatsou, Ollie Harris (again) and Ellie Rowley-Conwy, Sally Davis and Catherine Warren.

My family has showed me what unconditional love looks like. My numerous aunts, uncles and cousins were always there, looking over me when I needed it most.

Nothing would have been possible without my parents, Rafael and María José, my sister María Amalia and my brother-in-law Paco. This book means little to them, but they have enough knowing that it means the world to me. Therefore, I wish to dedicate this book to my nephew Julio and my niece Emma.

1

Introduction
Islam and Islamization

In this book I examine Islam in light of modern archaeological theory and propose a way to analyze Islamization from an archaeological point of view. My perspective is cultural: I seek to understand how Islam is felt and manifested in society. My suggestion is that the study of Islamization is a valid approach to this. As I explain in this text, I believe that Islamization is not the process by which Islam expands, but the process that results in Islam, and therefore the study of Islamization should be the key to understanding what different Islamic people and cultures have in common.

My approach to the issue is based on the consideration that Islamization is more about cultural change than conversion to Islam (without excluding it, of course). In principle, the definition of Islam seems to be more complicated than that of Islamization itself, as the former is a polysemic word that encompasses a wide range of historical, geographical, social and theological concepts with a large contextual dependence, while the latter can be understood as a particular kind of acculturation.

It is therefore acceptable to start this book by delimiting the range of meanings of Islam to the cultural sphere. In consequence, I will not discuss Islam from a theological or philosophical perspective, as this is a task that I consider myself unfit to attempt. This does not mean, of course, that I ignore the deep significance of Islam. My views are built upon a deep feeling of respect for the faith of the believers, but I explicitly build my arguments from a (new) materialist perspective without looking for any particular confirmation or rebuttal of Islamic belief. I do reject, however, any attempt to misconstrue Islamic religion, history, culture or institutions or the Muslims themselves from any stereotypical perspective. It may seem unnecessary to include this statement in an academic book, but unfortunately, we have seen on several occasions that academicism can be used to conceit Islamophobia and racism. At any rate I consider it important to state that my perspective as a non-Muslim does not diminish in any way my respect and awe for the history of Islamic societies. As a member of a multicultural European society, I regard Islam as my own past and heritage, as I hope will be made clear in the pages of this book.

This book is also about Islamic archaeology, and therefore a clarification on my use of the adjective 'Islamic' is in order. In line with my approach to Islam, the word in this text is always used in its sense of 'relative to Islam', and never as a chronological indicator unless explicitly stated. Sticking to this rule has forced me to use some awkward phrasing at times (e.g., 'early Islamic-period polity'), but I hope that the reader will excuse this because it allows me to be more precise. This, of course, affects to my own definition of 'Islamic archaeology' itself, which for me is more an 'archaeology of Islamic communities' than an 'archaeology of Islamic-period societies'.

In the following pages I will start to develop my argument with a review of the definitions of Islam and with an argument that will prove my point as to why Islamization is a key target for archaeological research if one intends to understand Islamic societies. I have chosen to start from that point because it allows me to develop the theoretical basis on which my perspective is built. An introduction to the topic of Islamic archaeology, or a brief account of the origins of Islam may have been more orthodox points of departure, but the inclusion of any of them in this chapter would have made it too long and would have required me to readdress and reconceptualize them in the following chapters. I trust that the reader will not need these sections until I tackle them in later parts of the book, but for those that require more information before starting this book, there are useful introductions to Islamic history (e.g. Ruthven 1997; Silverstein 2010) and Islamic archaeology (e.g. Milwright 2010).

What is Islam? I: Between belief and actuality

Anyone who attempts a definition of Islam will come to realize that the word Islam is polysemic, i.e. it includes a wide set of concepts that encompasses the religion of the Muslims and their way of life, and the historical and geographical scope of Muslims' influence. There is certainly a set of metonymical and metaphorical relationships between concepts at play here, and it is difficult to disentangle them from each other. It is for this reason that it is useful to start analyzing the historical development of the word Islam and the meanings associated with it. In order to do this, I will begin with the gold standard for the definition in the *Encyclopaedia of Islam*[1] elaborated by Louis Gardet (*EI2, s.v. Islam*: Vol 4: 171–4). Gardet addresses first the etymological background of the word. 'Islam' in English comes from the Arabic word *islām*, derived from the three-letter root *s-l-m*, which in Semitic language is associated with the ideas of wholeness, safety and peace. *Islām* is the verbal noun (*maṣdar*) of the form IV of the Arabic root *s-l-m*, and therefore it could be translated literally as 'entrusting one's safety to another'. An analysis of the way that the word is used in the Quran shows that in a religious context it has two complementary meanings: 'surrender to God' (as an inner, voluntary action) and 'profession of the religion' (*ibidem*: 171). Therefore, the earliest meaning of the word *islām* is well connected historically to the religion itself. How then, did it acquire other meanings?

The rest of the *EI* entry is based mainly on the work of Wilfred Cantwell Smith, a theologian and orientalist who studied lists of Islamic manuscripts and realized that the diverse ways of understanding Islam emerged in the context of intellectual debates among Muslim scholars in different time periods. In particular, he noticed the emergence of three meanings of the word in the history of Islam. The first one, present since the beginning, is directly based on the etymology of the word itself, as we have seen above: as *islām* is a *maṣdar*, a verbal noun, it refers to active personal faith. This is the meaning directly related to the individual's commitment with Islam as a religion. Given the importance of this definition, I have only sketched it here, and I will address it in more detail below after briefly presenting the other two definitions of Islam suggested by Cantwell Smith. These look at Islam as an institution, but in two different ways: one contemplates it as an ideal, as God's project; and the other considers it as an actuality, the result of humans' actions. This process of expanding the concept of Islam from active faith to first ideal and then actual institutions was labelled by Cantwell Smith as the 'reification' of Islam (1963: 75–108; 1981: 41–77).

The concept of Islam as an ideal project can be considered synonymous with the idea of *ummā* or a community of believers. It emerged more slowly and is closely connected to a term that was already in use in the Classical period of the Arabic Islamic tradition (eleventh to fourteenth centuries CE), that of *bilād al-Islām* (the Lands of Islam) or *dār al-Islām* (the Abode of Islam). The implication of these terms is that there is a unity in the Islamic community, even if it is politically fragmented, and despite the lack of a unified structure of religion, that unity is the acceptance of God's project. As described in the Quran, Islam is not 'a' religion, but *al-Dīn*, 'the' religion (*EI2*, Vol 4: 174), the final revelation that supersedes all former revelations (Judaism and Christianism), and the Prophet Muḥammad is the Seal of Prophets, the last one of all. Developments shortly after the beginning of their history, however, put Muslims in a wide range of cultural and political situations in which practical and varied answers were required. A share of this variety and pragmatism made its way through the nascent field of Islamic jurisprudence (*fiqh*), which, although based on the inscribed traditions of the Quran and the Hadith, became increasingly dependent on the contribution of different juridical schools. The reasoning and administration of law with this body of sources and institutions was systematized (although not closed to change) between the second and third centuries of Islam (eighth and ninth centuries CE). This systematization, however, is only a guide that covers the sources of the law and the way in which it must be interpreted, and so *fiqh*, Islamic jurisprudence, should not be understood as the blind application of a closed text, but rather as the exercise of interpreting the available sources with the aim of creating rules of law that can be used in particular situations (Schacht 1964: 6–75). As a result, although Muslims agree that God's project is one, it is not possible to pinpoint one single, particular, socio-political project that can be considered as representative of the whole Islamic community.

The last meaning of Islam being considered, that of the actuality of Islam as a result of humans' actions, was the characteristic perception of Islam by non-Muslim authors, that is, external observers, mostly translated European articles or works written by non-Muslim Arab natives between the late-nineteenth and early-twentieth centuries. European authors, in particular, abandoned former denominations, such as 'Mohammedanism' or 'Islamism' in favour of the term Islam, which they observed to be used by Muslim scholars (without grasping the difference between project and actuality that Cantwell Smith notes). These works, however, ended up having an impact on Muslim scholars, who adopted the new meaning of Islam to polemicize with former authors.

The analysis above can be qualified with two observations made by Gardet. The first of these is that the different concepts of Islam were prefigured in the first Islamic texts, and they went beyond mere potentialities as the original Islamic community expanded and was faced with other religious groups. The second observation is a consequence of the first one: the three meanings of Islam are very closely bound together and 'no study of Islam, no analysis of the Muslim community or of the world of Islam should separate them' (*EI2*, Vol 4: 174). This is an important note, as it reminds the reader that in Cantwell Smith's conception, any way of looking at Islam must ultimately refer to the original etymological definition of Islam and thus to a basic concept that is problematic from an archaeological point of view: faith.

The originality of Cantwell Smith's approach consists in that he was the first scholar to deny the essentialism of the concept of religion, the idea that there is a 'thing' called religion (1963). Despite that, he had a complicated conception of history and faith, which Talal Asad has criticized for hiding a form of that very same essentialism that he reacted against (Asad 2001). Cantwell Smith indeed rejected the idea of an Islam (or of any religion) as ontologically independent from history, but at the same time his own conception of history was based on a radical scepticism that led him to deny the ontology of all things in themselves except for the concepts of 'God' and 'Man'; in this scenario, therefore, things have qualities in relation to those concepts. 'Faith' is the connection between those two fundamental concepts, and therefore it is universal and transcendental, in opposition to the idea of 'religion,' which is a contingent reification of 'faith'. Asad looks at this question from a materialist perspective, and in consequence he does not share Cantwell Smith's philosophy. Following him, the main problem with Cantwell Smith's interpretation is that he is unable to separate faith and action, and therefore he does not define adequately the ways in which faith is enacted. Asad identifies Islam (and religion) not with the reflection of faith, but as the set of practices and discipline that make faith actual. He therefore defends a very different definition of Islam, one that considers faith from a perspective based on action and to which I will return to later in this argument. For the moment, however, I will stick with Cantwell Smith's thoughts about faith. Leaving aside the essentializing aspects of his approach, his work has an interesting outcome when it is applied to the definition of belief itself.

In his analysis of the Quran, Cantwell Smith noted that the word *islām* does not seem to correlate with the concept of faith particularly well (1981: 110–34). The word only appears eight times (*EI2*, Vol 4: 171), which has made scholars think that it was not a word particularly preferred above others when the text was written (and probably earlier). The idea of 'faith' is better associated to the word *īmān, maṣdar* of the root '-*m-n*, which has the connotations of 'being secure, trusting in, turning to' (this semitic root is also related to the word 'amen'). *Īmān* and its cognates are some of the most frequent occurrences in the sacred texts (Gardet in *EI2*, s.v. *Īmān*, Vol 3: 1170–4). Cantwell Smith explains that the concept of 'having faith' in this context needs a particular clarification, as it is not the same as that of 'believing'. The idea of belief in the Quran is closer to the concept of 'holding an opinion', whereas 'having faith' in the Quran is presented as a 'great drama of decision' (Cantwell Smith 1981: 122) in which humans are granted the knowledge of the truth and must act consequently: they obey or they rebel (Cantwell Smith 1981: 120–3). This is how the two concepts

Introduction: Islam and Islamization 7

of *islām* and *īmān* are clearly distinct yet closely connected in the Quran. The former implies a submission to God and active profession of that submission, and it is the origin of the word *muslim* (active participle of the verb *aslāmu* – 'to surrender' – and therefore translated as 'the person who surrenders to God'). The latter, instead, refers to the acceptance of the truth of the religion of Islam, and it is the origin of the word *mu'min* (active participle of the verb *a'manu*, – 'to have faith' – hence 'he who has faith', traditionally translated as 'believer'). This distinction opens the possibility that there were initially two accepted ways of manifesting submission to God, one being a firm believer (*mu'min*) and the other one accepting some ground rules of behaviour, while at the same time being somehow distant from the core belief (*muslim*). In fact, this difference has been the source of an interesting theory by Fred McGraw Donner, who suggested that the tension between *muslimūn* and *mu'minūn* (plural forms) was a pragmatic social arrangement at the core of the very first years of Islamic history before the two signifiers became synonyms around the end of the seventh century (Donner 2010). At the end of the century, the Quran was written down and there was an active theological and legal discussion on how to tackle this distinction (cf. the entries of *Islām* and *Īmān* in *EI2*). For Cantwell Smith, this opposition seems to have been just a mere etymological phenomenon that was corrected afterwards. Following Donner's example, I am more inclined to think that there was (and there is) an actual tension between the two words, and that it reflects the particular field created between belief and action where Muslims can find themselves. This reinforces Asad's criticism of Cantwell Smith's disinterest in action (as seen above) and should make us think of Islam in terms of the above mentioned field. The next section is therefore devoted to finding a definition of Islam around the concept of action.

What is Islam? II: Social practice, power and orthodoxy

In the section above I have explained Cantwell Smith's particular explanation of the polysemy of the word 'Islam', originally a concept emerging from a particular conception of the relationship between God and human beings through faith, and then 'reified' into other meanings more rooted on social dimensions and on historical actualities. This particular order of concepts is why Asad claims that the ideas of Cantwell Smith are essentializing: despite linking the concept of religion to history, the whole system is based on a transcendental concept of faith. For Asad, however, there is no faith outside historical circumstances. In his book *Genealogies of Religion* (1993), he rejects the concept of a religion as a transhistorical set of symbols that serve at the same time as a body of knowledge and as the trigger of people's emotions. Asad believes that this idea of religion is a Victorian concept that resulted in the particular historical development of Christianity. The early works of the fathers of Christianity were devoted to the careful definition of a body of beliefs that should be treated as the only true one. As a result of that, Christianity was developed as a body of texts that contained specific instructions to determine what was part of the religion and what was not, including in this not only matters of meaning and history, but also matters of ritual, performance and clarification on how emotions should be experienced in true Christian fashion. Afterwards, this well-defined conception of the religion of Christianity passed on to become the Victorian definition of a well-delimited concept of natural religion, and from there it was passed to anthropology (Asad 1993: 27–54). This obviously has a strong impact on the way in which we perceive a religion like Islam today. Islam is also considered to be a very structured and organized religion that happens to have fundamental differences with Christianity, not only in the dogmata, but in particular in the relations that it establishes with other structures in society. This has led to a common problem in the study of Islamic societies from the historical and the anthropological points of view: the consideration of religion as a particular sphere of culture, which in theory can be isolated and studied separately. Somehow paradoxically, this led some scholars to take an essentialist form of Islam as determining of the shape of all other social institutions and even individual agency.

As an anthropologist, Asad is particularly critical of this problem in the attempts to define an anthropology of Islam. In an article written in 1986 (republished in 2009 with slight editions), he develops this criticism by focusing on the reflections of two eminent scholars whose works are very influential: Ernest Gellner (and particularly his book *Muslim Society*, 1981) and Clifford Geertz (specifically his *Islam Observed*, 1968, which is also the object of similar criticism by Varisco 2005). Gellner's book is based on his description of the society of Morocco as essentially divided into two traditions of Islam, one orthodox and another one heterodox, based respectively in cities and the countryside. Geertz noticed a different yet similar tension between a rigorous and puritan Islam in Moroccan tradition and a more syncretic and flexible one in Indonesia. Although the functionalist approach of Gellner and the structuralist anthropology of Geertz represents opposing schools of thought in anthropology, Asad considers that they both make the same mistake when defining a model of Islam in Morocco that afterwards is universalized as a paradigm: they consider the development of Islam as a social drama where Muslims do not have agency, only behaviour. In both models, Muslims are actors playing prefigured roles, city-dwellers or tribesmen, and are at the same time holders of distinctive forms of Islam, one based on textual orthodoxy and a religious hierarchy, another one based on heterodox views inspired by local saints. In these representations there is no space for sedentary peasants, for example, who are absolutely absent of these dramatic narratives, or indeed there is no consideration of the political economies that form the basis of societies. The construction of these perspectives is based on a Western (European) professional writing tradition that originates in the French 'sociology of Islam' and that was enriched (particularly by Gellner) with excerpts extracted from classical works of sociology of religion (e.g. Marx, Weber, Durkheim), British segmentary theory and selected extracts from the *Muqaddimah* of Ibn Khaldūn. To a certain extent, this means that Gellner and Geertz conceived their own proposals for an anthropology of Islam as statements within a particular field of studies that had been developed before them. In other words, they adopted the scope and limitations of this field in their own theoretical constructions. In contrast, by eliminating the constraints imposed by a concept of natural religion, Asad forces us to consider faith as a matter of practice, discourse and power in societies.

The alternative proposal of Asad inverts the relationship between Islam and society. Rather than defining Islam first and then adjusting social structures to fit with it, Asad reclaims the embeddedness of Islam within the communities where Muslims live. In other words, he rejects any cultural apriorism in the definition of local Islam and focuses on the study of political economies to understand relationships of production and of power. In this perspective, faith is not merely an acceptance of the belief in something, but a practice built around a set of disciplinary measures and concepts held and defended by a discursive tradition that is historically linked to the founding texts of the Quran and the Hadith. 'An Islamic discursive tradition is simply a tradition of Muslim discourse that addresses itself to conceptions of the Islamic past and future, with reference to a particular Islamic tradition in the present' (Asad 2009: 20). It is therefore an 'instituted practice' that defines the orthodoxy of Islamic doctrine and practice (*ibidem*: 21); orthodoxy in this context is 'a relation of power to the truth' (*ibidem*: 22). And the way in which this power is exercised, its constraining and enabling circumstances, the way in which individuals use it or are influenced by it, should be the object of an anthropology of Islam.

At this point it is useful to consider, with some detail, where Asad's thoughts are leading us. He offers a clearer, more self-contained definition of an anthropology of Islam by establishing a neat separation between social formation, which is ultimately dependent on its political economy and relations of production, and Islam, which is defined as a discursive tradition embedded in society. On the other hand, however, the definition of discursive tradition is linked to that of orthodoxy, which is itself related to power by definition. This means that the separation between Islam and society cannot be absolute, because the issue of power lies at the bottom of both of them. It is also worth noting that despite marked differences, Asad's perspectives resonate strongly with Cantwell Smith's ideas, since the relationship between discourse/orthodoxy and action mirrors the tension between belief and action that was discussed above. In order to explore these issues, it is necessary to open up the discussion of Islam to the question of social practice.

The definition of discursive tradition as an instituted practice also has a strong resonance with the concepts used by Pierre Bourdieu in his works on practice theory ([1972] 1977; [1980] 1990). For Bourdieu, the key concept to understanding social practice is *habitus*, a generative principle of social production and reproduction by which individuals learn how the society in which they live is organized and how their agency can be effective in obtaining particular results, either to keep the status quo or to alter it. The sense of social organization that the habitus transmits is what Bourdieu termed the *doxa*, the common accepted ground for social development (i.e. the experience of 'what is taken for granted' in social debate). In this scenario, the discursive tradition conceived by Asad plays a double role in that it is contained in its definition as 'instituted practice', making it work at the same time as a discursive device of social bonding and as an extended field of concepts that form part of the *doxa*. From the perspective of practice, individuals consciously engage in this discursive tradition, mainly to be educated, but also to clarify, discuss and understand aspects of the Islamic tradition that are relevant in their lives. As an institution, the discursive tradition makes Islamic orthodoxy, i.e. the relationship of power to the truth, part of the *doxa*, so that it becomes naturally embedded in *habitus* and is thus (re)produced in social practice.

What is Islam? III: Structuration agency and theory

The work of Asad seen through the lens of Bourdieu opens the door to consider the definition of Islam from the perspective of archaeological theory. Adopted by the energetic stream of postprocessual archaeological thought from at least the end of the 1990s, the ideas of practice and its correlate agency (see below) have permeated archaeology (Harris and

Cipolla 2017: 35–51). However, despite Bourdieu's experience in North Africa, where many of his theories took shape, his work has not inspired any particular approaches to Islam. Instead, there has been one particular archaeological approach to Islam that has been grounded on a sociological theory that emerged at the same time as Bourdieu's practice theory, and that can be considered its mirror image in most aspects. The theory to which I am referring here is structuration theory, formulated by Anthony Giddens in his *Constitution of Society* (1984), and the approach to Islam based on it in Tim Insoll's *Archaeology of Islam* (1999).

Structuration theory conceives societies as a combination of social institutions and individual action. The agency of the individuals is at the same time constrained and enabled by the institutions, but these are, in turn, structures that are susceptible to historical change because of the unintended consequences of individual action. The parallels with Bourdieu's theory are evident, but whereas practice theory is focused on the conditions that shape practice (which we could roughly define as the materialization of agency in Giddens' terminology), structuration theory aims to analyze the ways in which agency generates and changes social structures. In archaeological thought, it is frequent to see both theories used to develop perspectives on agency, separately or even together. In this discussion, however, it is necessary to focus now on structuration theory, which inspired Insoll's perspectives on Islam.

Insoll adopted structuration theory to analyze the complexities of Islamic societies in a way that made it amenable to archaeological research. In his view, Islam should be understood as a superstructure made of core principles that provide the foundations for a substructure composed of the different material manifestations of those principles (1999: 1). With his theory, Insoll is echoing the tension between different manifestations of Islam that had been noted by anthropologists (*ibidem*: 9–11). However, Insoll explicitly refers to Ferdinand Braudel's distinction between the change rhythms in *longue dureé, conjonctures* and *événements* as a way of explaining the differences between superstructure and substructure in his view of Islam (*ibidem*: 12–13). In this way, Insoll's theory is built on a framework of structures subjected to different patterns of historical time that reflect Gidden's thoughts about social constitution, agency and structuration. Insoll's perspective on Islam, therefore, steps away from the behaviourism of anthropological representations and at the same time presents a bold new idea from the point of view of archaeology: Islam, as a superstructure, has not a single manifestation, but many possible different ones, which are, in turn, structural to the societies of which they are part.

A very relevant difference emerges as soon as one compares Asad's and Insoll's perspectives on Islam. Although the former locates it in social practice, the latter considers it as part of structures. Nevertheless, a closer look at Insoll's perspective on religious views shows that he is as sceptical to a Victorian, isolated definition of religion as Asad is (cf. Insoll 2004: 6–8). This does not mean that his approach to faith, and in particular to Islam, is similar to Asad's, who states that faith must be defined in relation to an orthodoxy established on disciplinary and discursive practices embedded in society (2009). Insoll instead suggests that we should think of belief as an influential factor in the form of realities, such as economies, politics, social institutions, etc. (2004: 22–3). Despite this difference, Insoll's archaeology of Islam is interested precisely in the same kind of objectives that Asad's anthropology of Islam is: the study of the social practices that transmit and reflect Islamic doctrine in the daily life of Muslims. And this is not the only thing these two approaches have in common.

Asad and Insoll conceive the root of Islam to be a core set of beliefs that are central to faith. Beyond this, there is a discursive tradition for Asad and a set of super- and substructures of principles for Insoll. What both conceptions fail to show is how the wide diversity of Islamic practices emerge from this root of core beliefs, which is a result of the historical and material relationships established by Muslims in different moments of their history. This history – it is important to remember – is not only determined by Islamic structures. In the case of Insoll's theory, the variety of Islamic practices is considered as part of the structure, but the definition is insufficient because the core of Islamic principles is not affected by historical change, or in a very different way that the material substructures.

This means that there is not a clear explanation of how the different levels of structures (core superstructure, material substructures) are integrated historically. This makes Insoll's definition a valid model to explain what Islam can potentially be, but problematic when it comes to understand what it is, the actual reasons for its multiple forms. Asad's perception of Islam is less problematic with regard to history, since the discursive tradition that embodies it is deeply embedded in specific historical social formations. However, other problems emerge. In defining orthodoxy as a relationship of power to the truth, Asad roots Islam in the authority of a social group composed of religious specialists trained in specific practices and discourses. It is unclear from this perspective how different traditions and divergent orthodoxies can be formed, as it does not seem to be in the nature of the discursive practice to allow the proliferation of division. It can be argued that Asad regards the relationship of knowledge established between individuals and tradition as one possible source of Islamic variety, because he makes it clear that tradition is not a mere acceptance of the teachings received by the specialist, but that it encompasses a process of convincing that requires explanations, arguments and demonstrations (2009: 20–2). However, it remains a problem to understand what the sources of resistance to tradition may be. Surely if individuals need to be won over for tradition, by necessity they were holding a different view beforehand. The chances are that at least part of these challenging views did not have their origin in an established Islamic tradition, but they are products of the interactions of Muslims with their historical circumstances. It is interesting to note that in Asad's and Insoll's definitions of Islam the role of history is taken for granted, and yet kept beyond the boundaries of the definition itself. In other words, these two theoretical views on Islam have rejected the essentialism that was lurking behind the concept of faith of Cantwell Smith, and have supported a vision of Islam on the pillars of social practice and structuration; and yet, paradoxically, they have both found themselves in the need to establish a sort of *faux* essentialism, a space where an eternal return to the fundamentals of faith is possible and supported by the same structures and practices that are continuously changing with history.

I believe that the history of Islam, or more precisely, the history of the Muslims, needs to be included in any definition of Islam if this is to be operative from the point of view of disciplines such as anthropology or archaeology. It is simply not enough to assume that Islam is linked to history; Islam is essentially the history of the connection of Muslims with their core beliefs. However, Muslims are also shaped by their interaction with their historical and material circumstances, including their relationships with non-Muslims. A socio-cultural study of Islam, or better, the study of an Islamic society, should aim to comprehend all these conditions in their own historical context. As a consequence of this, Islamization should not be merely understood as the spread of Islam in society, although this definition may be correct in certain cases. A more accurate definition of Islamization, however, is the process by which a set of historical conditions come together to generate Islamic history, or in definitive, Islam.

The importance of being Islamic

A recent work has explored the relationships of Islam with the history of Muslims, while at the same time offering an original and interesting view on the dichotomy between faith and action presented above. I am referring here to Shahab Ahmed's work *What is Islam? The Importance of Being Islamic* (2016), where Islam is presented as a field that is at the same time the medium and the result of the hermeneutical engagement of believers with the Revelation of God to Muḥammad in the world. In this way, Ahmed (a Muslim himself) accepts the premise of transcendental belief posed by Cantwell Smith, while also introducing a principle of action and structure in Islam itself.

For Ahmed, Muslims are active seekers of meaning in the world, and Islam is at the same time their medium, or common language for this search, and the result of it. Faith, therefore, consists in the acceptance of the Revelation as part of the world to be explored, without a commitment to a particular teleological or moral end. The most recognized field of this exploration is exegetic, and consists of the hermeneutics of the sacred texts of the Islamic tradition (what Ahmed calls 'the Text'). Beyond that, however, Ahmed contends that there is a non-textual, more mundane field of exploration – which he calls 'Pre-Text' – where the Revelation is engaged in philosophy, science, politics, arts, crafts and in everyday activities. This engagement is, it must be remembered, hermeneutic, not dictated by an externally imposed orthodoxy. This means that Muslims are continuously generating Islamic meaning, and within it, a range of interpretations, disagreements and even contradictions. However, all these meanings can be found to '*disagree meaningfully*', as Ahmed puts it (2016: 292), and this is because they are all immersed in Islam. Of course, these hermeneutics are historically bound to their context, and this is where Ahmed introduces his concept of Con-Text. With this word, Ahmed defines '*the whole field or complex or vocabulary of meanings of Revelation that have been produced in the human and historical hermeneutical engagement with Revelation* and which are thus *already present as Islam*' (*ibidem*: 356, Italics in the original). Therefore, Con-Text is both the medium and the result of the hermeneutical engagement of Muslims with the Revelation, whether in the fields of Text or of Pre-Text. If we 'reify' the religion in Cantwell Smith's sense, we can even simplify and identify Con-Text with Islam itself.

    The work of Ahmed is particularly relevant because it considers Islam from the perspective of a Muslim familiar both with his own Pakistani Islamic cultural background (what he calls the Balkans-to-Bengal cultural complex, encompassing the historical inheritance of the Ottoman, Persian and Mughal Empires), but also with the different academic traditions that have studied Islam from legal, religious, historical and anthropological perspectives (very little of archaeology, though, which highlights the need of archaeologists to engage). He analyzes and criticizes them extensively and he underlines what he perceives as the two major misinterpretations of Islam from the point of view of the Western academic gaze: the separation between religious and secular spheres and the tendency to conceive Islam as prescriptive. Ahmed indicates that in pre-modern Islamic contexts the separation between secular and religious life constitutes an abusive imposition on societies where this conception did not exist. Although he is echoing Asad's criticism of the Victorian concept of religion, Ahmed believes that Asad is ultimately guilty of the same separation precisely because of his ring-fencing of Islam to the orthodoxy that is the product of a discursive tradition, ultimately dominated by scholars specialized in prescription (*ibidem*: 270-5). The emphasis on prescription and normative constraints over creative engagements is precisely the other problem. As a Muslim who is particularly well aware of the cultural richness of Islamic culture, Ahmed finds that there is much exploration and curiosity rooted on Islam, and yet secularist observers tend to set them apart.

The criticism of Ahmed is extremely relevant and will be referred to in different parts of the text. His hermeneutic conception of Islam has inspired much of the approach to Islamization that follows, although there are relevant additions and liberties taken with his work that will be duly noted. In particular, an effort has been made to conciliate Ahmed's work with recent posthumanist archaeological theory.

Islam, archaeological theory and Islamization

In the section above, I have redefined the concept of Islam as 'history'. But this is not simply the history of the Muslims as a mere succession of objective facts. It is the history of all Islamic beings, human and not-human alike, in their search for the meaning of the Revelation of God to the Prophet Muḥammad. I am not claiming that this is the only possible account of the past. My claim is rather that accepting the existence of this past in the present is the only way to reach an understanding of what Islam is.

I can digress briefly on the concept of history that I am using here. My notion of history does not refer only to the past, but to the continuum of relationships between humans and non-humans across time and space (in fact, giving sense to time and space, as I will explain). This definition of history owes much to posthumanist thinking, which I introduce with some detail in Chapter 4. For the moment, this definition of Islam as history means that it has two important characteristics. One is that Islam is a multidimensional entity that cannot be perceived in its totality by any observer. However, it can be 'projected' or 'modelled', so that some of its dimensions can be examined from particular perspectives that sacrifice the perception of some other dimensions (just like the same tridimensional object can be represented with different bidimensional projections depending on the perspective taken by the observer). Some of the ways in which Islam can be modelled are structural principles, social practices or even particular projects and actualities of Islam. In this way, the perspectives taken by Cantwell Smith, Asad and Insoll that I have examined above are not necessarily wrong but show only a part of the totality of dimensions that Islam can encompass. As Gardet encouraged the readers of *EI* with regard to the different meanings of Islam identified by Cantwell Smith, it is necessary to remember that all these perspectives can be analyzed in themselves, but we should never try to separate them (*EI2*, Vol 4: 174). Ahmed, with his definition of Con-Text, offers a way to consider them in a relationship of commensurability within Islam as a historical development.

The other characteristic of Islam, one which is even more relevant for the purposes of this book, is that it is the result of very specific and particular entanglements between humans and non-humans across space and time, all together forming the history of the Muslims. We can see now that the very same definition of Islam as the history of the Muslims is incomplete, since Islam encompasses also the history of things, animals, plants, etc. that are related to the Muslims in the networks of relationships that shape Islam. And not only that: Islam encompasses also the history of people who are not necessarily Muslims, but whose lives are very much entangled in the networks of this particular history. This is a point worth emphasizing: the networks that shape Islam do not only include Muslims or things intimately related to Islamic practice (such as a mosque or a copy of the Quran); they also encompass non-Muslims and things that are not related to Islamic practice or belief. In other words, the quality of being a Muslim person or an inherently Islamic thing is not a necessary condition to be entangled in the networks that form Islam; on the contrary, these networks include many people and things that do not have this quality in themselves, but that are relevant or necessary parts of the network because they contribute to making it sustainable and actual. As we will see, being Islamic consists in being part of that network. In the same way that Islam is shaped by a network of humans and non-humans that have their qualities constituted by their relationships, the quality of being Islamic is acquired though the entanglement in particular relationships that may or may not be active during their whole biographical trajectory. This is where the definition of Islamization comes in useful and becomes adequate for archaeological theory. Islamization is not only the study of how people become Muslims, but is also the study of the entanglements of Islam with people and things. The study of Islamization is the way in which we can study the specific relationships of different individuals, communities and things with the network of Islam. From this perspective, the concepts of Islam and Islamization are not limited to Muslims, but they can be used in an expanded method of analysis to elucidate the meaning of particular identities, communities and localized networks with their entanglement in a wider network, allowing the understanding of the uniqueness of each of them in their own context.

In the chapters that follow I will make my views on Islamization more explicit, by examining particular aspects of the mesh of relationships that define Islam. Before going into this level of detail, however, it is necessary to review other approaches to Islam that I seek to improve on in light of this theoretical perspective. Therefore, in Chapter 2 I will summarize briefly the history of Islamic archaeology and explore several ways in which Islamization has been considered from the point of view of historians and archaeologists. In Chapter 3 I will explore ideas related to Islamic identity in relation to Muslims, and in particular the views of anthropologist Gabrielle Marranci. In these two chapters I develop a critique of the ideas most frequently held about Islam and Islamization using the monumental work of Shahab Ahmed.

In Chapter 4 I turn to new materialist and posthumanist theory to develop a new approach. Here I take into account the criticism raised by Ahmed on current scholarship on Islam and build on the philosophy of Giles Deleuze. Following the lead of recent works in archaeological theory, I propose a reconsideration of what Islamic beings are, which has very important implications for the understanding of Islam and Islamization from the perspective of a non-Muslim person. In Chapter 5 I propose two examples of the application of my ideas, based on case studies of my own work.

Chapter 6 is the conclusion of this work, where different views on Islamization raised at different parts of this book, in different debates covered by the text, are gathered together. In this chapter I also close my work by offering some final thoughts on what my definitions of Islam and Islamization imply. Although posthumanist, my theoretical approach does not intend to erase Muslims and other Islamic human beings from history, nor to build an interpretation of history that can supersede all others, Muslim or not. Rather, this is an attempt to engage in a consideration of the past that is not determined only by Western and humanist concepts and that aspires to learn and become widened by engagement with Islamic views.

2

Islamization

From Conversion to Cultural Change

Islamic archaeology and Islamization

The discipline of Islamic archaeology is a relatively young field, but it has a long history. In its earliest version, modern studies about the material culture of the Islamic world started almost at the same time as the first analysis of classical archaeology emerged. By the eighteenth century, European enlightened intellectuals showed interest in the compilation of inscriptions from Arabic epigraphy and coinage, as the works of George Kehr in 1724 and Carsten Niebuhr in 1774, among others, indicate (Milwright 2010: 12). The patron behind the first excavations in Herculaneum in 1738, King Charles V of Naples and Sicily, later sponsored, as King Charles III of Spain, the first European study of Islamic antiquities, published in the two volumes of *Antigüedades Árabes de España* (1787 and 1804) (Almagro Gorbea 2015; Almagro Gorbea and Maier Allende 2012). During the late-nineteenth century and early-twentieth century, imperialist and colonialist interests were behind archaeological excavations of Islamic-period sites in Iberia and North Africa by France and Spain (De Beylié 1909; Velázquez Bosco 1912; 1922–1923), in the Middle East (including Egypt and Persia) by the Ottoman and German Empires, Great Britain and France (Gabriel 1920; Vernoit 1997: 3–4; Sarre and Hertzfeld 1911–1920; Yoltar-Yildirim 2013) and in Central Asia by Russia (first Imperial, and afterwards Soviet) (Tikhonov 2007).[1] If imperialism made these explorations possible, Orientalism was the main paradigm of interpretation (Said 1978), and much of it remained in place well after archaeological research became the responsibility of decolonized states in the second half of the twentieth century (Vernoit 1997: 6–8). This could be seen in a disproportionate interest for descriptions of art and architecture and a corresponding lack of attention paid to questions of social and economic analysis (correlated with a lack of care for the protection and documentation of archaeological levels related to Islamic-period material culture in multiphasic sites) (Milwright 2010: 6). One of the most pervasive tenets of Orientalism was that the 'Oriental' mind is essentially different to the 'Western' mind, and this was translated in a number of stereotypical assumptions about Orientals in general and Muslims in particular (Vernoit 1997: 1; Said 1978). Islamic archaeology and history were no exception. Consequently, Islamization, the search for an understanding of cultural and social change under Islam, was not a question in the agenda of scholarship.

Islamic archaeology underwent methodological renovation in the second half of the twentieth century, but mostly as the end receiver of a range of related fields in different aspects, especially art history, architecture, landscape archaeology and historical archaeology (Milwright 2010: 17–20). During most of this time, the name 'Islamic archaeology' was exclusively associated with art historical and architectural studies (cf. Grabar 1971; 1976), and was generally ignored by mainstream archaeologists. The discipline of Islamic archaeology as a unified and recognized field did not start until around the end of the twentieth century (Walker et al 2020a: 1).[2] Despite these advances, archaeologists have not yet developed a specific theoretical approach to Islamization. This means that Islamization is understood as a loose concept of expansion of Islam, which could be used in relation to religion, to culture or both. It is usually applied in particular in early Islamic-period contexts, to understand religious conversion and cultural change as triggered by the Arab conquests of the seventh to ninth centuries (cf. Fenwick 2019; Walmsley 2007; Walker et al 2020a: 7; Walker et al 2020b: in particular Sections II and III).

Archaeology has counted with conceptual tools to propose different concepts of Islamization at least since the 1990s, such as the post-structuralist critiques to the processualist project. *The Archaeology of*

Islam of Tim Insoll (1999) was a suggestive first attempt in this direction. The book was critical of the traditional problems of Islamic archaeology, which Insoll characterized as excessively focused on stereotypes and in need of theoretical and methodological renovations to overcome its conception as an ancillary discipline to art historical studies (*ibidem*: 3–7). The next statement on the discipline, Marcus Milwright's *An Introduction to Islamic Archaeology* (2010), recognized the need for methodological renovation, but it was also a response to Insoll and a defence of the culture-historical approach to Islamic archaeology to some extent. Unlike Insoll, Milwright was optimistic about the status of Islamic archaeology, which has manifestly improved from the point of view of processes and methodologies. He was also sceptical about Insoll's proposal regarding the religious archaeology of Islam, choosing to define Islamic archaeology as a contingent discipline that analyzes very different societies that have developed under the rule of Islamic elites (*ibidem*: 6–9). The opposition between these works of Insoll and Milwright in the first decades of the twenty-first century illustrates the two considerations among which the concept of Islamization can be found in archaeology, which could be roughly identified as religious and cultural (cf. Walker et al. 2020a: 7).

In the rest of this chapter, I am going to explore the paradigms of humanities associated with these two considerations, religious and cultural, and the problems that they raise. I will depart from the issues that a lack of Islamization theory generates and will then discuss different perspectives used by historians and archaeologists. The selection of authors does not imply that their reflections are particularly deserving of criticism. On the contrary, I think that these works are worthy of attention for their ability to highlight relevant issues concerning the relationship of Islamization with conversion and with cultural change.

Islamization as mass conversion

When Islamization is first considered, it is generally identified as the religious transformation of a population. A good way to ponder the problems associated with the concept of Islamization as conversion is to review the theories that have been designed to account for how the phenomenon can take place. The circumstances and conditions of any historical process of mass conversion are of course very varied, depending on the period and region considered, but it is possible to generalize a few models that can summarize the main causal lines among which the theories are developed. An excellent introduction to this is the work of Richard Eaton on the Islamization of East Bengal (1993), which occurred under the Mughal domination of India. Although I will focus on Eaton's particular conclusions about Bengal later in the text, for the moment I am only interested in his introduction to the problem, which summarizes the theories of Islamization (as mass conversion) in India (*ibidem*: 113–19). This spawned a long period of time, and therefore it could be observed and commented on by colonial administrators and British and Indian scholars alike between the sixteenth and the twentieth centuries. As a result of this, there is an abundance of written and material documentation about the process of Islamization, and it has even given rise to literature trying to account for it. Eaton observed that the main theories drawn to explain how the Hindi population converted focused on the characteristics that Islam had as a religion and were usually reasoned along the lines of one or several of four models.

The first model considered is the Immigration model, which suggests that all or most Muslims in India are descendants of the Companions of the Prophet. Their ancestors migrated at some point to India either through the Iranian plateau or via the Arabian sea. This is an unsustainable claim, but this model of Islamization resonates in many societies where elites were interesting in linking themselves with the descents of the Prophet or of their companions; the adaptation or confection of genealogies is not something infrequent in Islamic contexts, particularly in situations where social capital can be acquired in this way.[3] Eaton sensibly rejects this model as a useful one to explain Islamization (*ibidem*: 113).

The second model, Religion of the Sword, suggests that Islamization was the result of a process of forced conversion by an armed body of invaders. The exact procedure by which a compulsory conversion is achieved is never explained satisfactorily, as in this model there is an emphasis on the more expansive and aggressive aspects and interpretations of Islamic doctrines as a cause of Islamization, but never an analysis of the historical procedures to achieve the feat of conversion by compulsion. This was a theory developed by European colonial administrators, who favoured an Orientalist perception of the Islamic civilization in general, and in the sultanates of India in particular. Another reason to be distrustful of this model is the distribution of the Muslim population in India. As Eaton rightfully remarks, a model like this would imply that concentrations of Muslims live in the places where the pressure for their conversion could be exerted, that is, in the seats of power of Islamic dynasties. But the highest concentrations of Muslims in India happen to be in the fringes of the areas under Islamic domination, such as East Bengal or Western Punjab, far away from centres of power in the Ganges valley, such as Delhi or Agra.

The third one of Eaton's models, Religion of Social Patronage, considers that the Hindi population converted because of the perspective of gaining some social or material benefit from the ruling class of India with their conversion. There is certainly some historical evidence for this process in the texts of Ibn Baṭṭūṭah and in the cases of several social groups in India, but it again fails to account for the mass conversions that took place in Punjab and Bengal, where most Muslims are from poor rural classes.

And finally, the model of Religion of Social Liberation was proposed by British ethnographers and historians, and was then adopted by many in Pakistan and Bangladesh, and by many Muslim historians of South Asia. In this case, the theory focuses on the aspects of egalitarianism of Islamic doctrines, which contrast starkly with the Hindu caste system. Whereas this is a more benign interpretation of Islam (not so much of Hinduism), it is still a simplification that is not supported by strong historical evidence. There is no record of a search for social egalitarianism in Hindi communities, and Islamic intellectuals stressed religious equality, but did not question the social order until the nineteenth century at least, under the influence of reformers who had absorbed and digested the ideas of Enlightenment. The distribution of Muslims in the Indian subcontinent is not favourable to this theory either. One would suppose that the Model of Social Liberation would be most effective in areas where the caste system of India was more firmly established, but these areas are again far away from Punjab and Bengal, which were peripheral areas with respect to the great centres of Brahmanic civilization.

The review Eaton makes of these theories is his main justification to address his study of the Islamization of East Bengal from a different perspective, which I analyze below. For the moment, however, I would like to dwell more on the discussion about these models of Islamization, as I feel that they are useful to describe a more general approach to Islamization as mass conversion that has characterized the study of Islamic societies in general and of archaeology in particular.

The first criticism that these models raise is the simplistic characterization that they make of Islam and of Hinduism, which becomes reduced to a few features used to explain how they succeeded or failed to attract converts. This reduction is problematic because it does not recognize the complexity of these systems of beliefs and their flexibility under different historical circumstances.

The second problem is even more difficult to solve. When analyzed in detail, the models above suggest that there are two major forces driving the acceptance of Islam: fear of brute force or a search for political or economic benefit. This raises the significant problem of sincerity of individual conversion: how can we believe that conversion is sincere if it is done by fear or by greed? Can it be considered conversion at all? It is not possible to analyze conversion from the point of view of its cause, of a particular reason that can explain the decision of individuals to convert to Islam from another religion, without ultimately questioning its sincerity, and therefore the action of conversion itself.

Islamization and conversion to Islam in scholarly studies

The problem of the sincerity of conversion has been highlighted when analyzing the syncretic nature of many conversions to Islam, which would be considered insincere from the point of view of Christian conversion (DeWeese 1995: 26, also noted in Peacock 2016b: 4–5). The point that followed was the recommendation that conversion to Islam should not be understood under the same light as conversion to Christianity, which requires a total acceptance of the faith dogmata contained in its doctrine. This is not the case in Islamic theological discussions, which are more open to the concept of syncretism than Christianity; they do not conceive the possibility of a formal and insincere acceptance of Islam, because they believe that formal acceptance of Islam will inevitably lead to belief.[4]

From my point of view, however, the problem is wider than a different perception between Christian and Islamic doctrine. The problem of conversion is the paradox of trying to find a cause for it outside of conversion itself. I do not think that this problem is exclusively related to Islamic faith. With very few exceptions, anybody who is questioned for the causes of their most intimate identity (be it religious, national, sexual or whatsoever) would be puzzled and unable to offer an answer that is not self-referential (e.g. 'it is my belief', 'it is my upbringing', 'it is my birth condition') or absolute (e.g. 'it is the truth'). This does not mean that social identities cannot be rationally questioned, but that for the immense majority of people, changes in social identity are not the result of rational choices, but of the acceptance of certain circumstances as a defining part of life, which can be afterwards reasoned in different ways. Human beings are not rational beyond or despite their social identities, but within them, because the idea of humanity itself is historically produced (cf. Barrett 2014).[5]

Therefore the quest for a cause for conversion should not be the key to understanding Islamization. To be sure, conversion is an individual process that cannot be explained, it can only be reasoned by taking into consideration the circumstances in which it is produced. The research on Islamization should not focus exclusively on the advantages that Islam as a religion brings, but on the changes implemented in the social system of the communities where an Islamic society is installed, and on how these changes configure the relationships of these communities with the rest of Islamic communities in their time and in history. It is important to be explicit that this study should include communities and individuals that do not convert to Islam. The expansion of Islamic communities brought many changes into the cultures it reached regardless of conversion. It is therefore easy to see that this is a process that goes well beyond individual conversion.

The fact that the concept of Islamization is still strongly linked to the idea of conversion and has experienced almost no changes since it became problematized, is telling of the lack of intellectual interest in this issue. In fact, the concept of Islamization is not even discussed in any of the three editions of the *Encyclopaedia of Islam*. In the most recent comparative work, the monumental *Islamisation* edited by Andrew Peacock (2016a), the editor recognizes that the most commonly accepted meaning of Islamization in scholarship is linked to the idea of conversion (Peacock 2016b: 1–4). Peacock also notes that in the first comparative study of Islamization (Levtzion 1979), there is no discussion about its meaning, and this implies that the only difference between conversion and Islamization is that the former refers to the individual and the latter to the accumulative effects of individual conversion. For other scholars in Peacock's edited volume, Islamization is recognized as a much wider process, which implies the establishment of a society regulated by Islamic norms. A similar but distinct meaning is emphasized by scholars who look at more culture-related aspects of the term, related to the establishment of clear markers of Islam in an area (such as mosques or madrasas) or the adoption of non-explicitly-Islamic things that can be used as vehicles of Islamization in particular historical contexts (such as the Arabic language or Iranian ideas of kingship). At the end of his discussion, however, Peacock recognizes the difficulty of defining specifically what Islamization is and decides to return to the idea of conversion as the starting point to reach an understanding of it (Peacock 2016b: 4).

Islamization beyond conversion

In the following pages I am going to present two case studies of Islamization that go some way beyond the definition of conversion. They present interesting ideas that allow us to consider the concept from a more cultural point of view.

The early Islamic-period world: The curve of conversion

The first case of Islamization considered here is the one developed by Richard Bulliet in his work *Conversion to Islam in the Medieval Period* (1979). Despite the title, which does not specifically mention Islamization, this book offers important insights on the concept, because the author specifically starts with a statement indicating that conversion to Islam must necessarily be related to the creation of an Islamic society (*ibidem*: 1). In this book, Bulliet proposes an ingenuous quantitative model to approximate the rate of conversion to Islam of the people inhabiting the countries under Islamic dominion during the first centuries after the takeover. The data to build the model are taken from genealogical lists contained in biographical dictionaries, a popular literary genre in the Islamic societies under consideration, where famous scholars were listed, and their genealogies described until their first memorable ancestor. Bulliet reasoned that that person would be the first ancestor in the lineage to have converted to Islam. This could be confirmed by analyzing the names of the genealogy; usually the first name of the list was not Arab or Muslim, but all their descendants would have Arab or Muslim names. With this information, Bulliet was able to count the generations passed after the first conversion in the family and calibrate the number of years that had gone by between the conversions and the compilation of the dictionaries. After this was done for all the genealogical lists of a country, Bulliet observed that the dates of conversions threw a consistent pattern that could be plotted on different sets of systems of Cartesian coordinates to be analyzed. The most famous representation of Bulliet's work is the cumulative curve of conversion, plotted over a coordinate system with time in the horizontal axis and the percentage of converted in the vertical axis. The result was an S-curve, so-called because it could be divided into four distinctive parts that represented major stages of the rates of conversion. The first part, where the lower branch of the S takes off, is a convex curve that represents the period in which Islam was only adopted by a small number of people; the second and third stages feature the highest rates of conversion, the second part of the curve being convex and the third part being concave; finally, the fourth and last stage of the graph is a concave curve where the rate of conversion decreases as the laggards are still adopting Islam.

Not only did the S-curve represent a consistent pattern of genealogical data, but the chronological distribution of the separation of phases in every region also matched with more or less accuracy the dates of important events in the Islamic history of the regions under consideration (for example, political changes in Iran, Iraq, Syria and Iberia). This suggests that the changes in conversion rates reflect changes in the balance of power between different social groups and that to a certain extent they were part of deep causes of major historical events.

The pattern of changes in conversion rates, however, was not influenced by political events, according to Bulliet; the repeated S-curve in different regions of the early Islamic-period world suggested that there was an underlying set of causes for this. The S-curve pattern of growth had been detected first in biological studies of population growth and then it had been transferred to studies of technological diffusion. In biological studies, the S-pattern was associated with changes in the rates of reproduction associated with the demographic growth of species in an environment with a limited amount of resources.[6] In the technological diffusion studies, the key element to explain the pattern was the flow of information about a new technique that improved work processes. At the start of the sequence, only a small numbers of users had access to a new technique and therefore its spread rate was low; as the number of users with access to the technique increased, the flow of information about it expanded and it was more rapidly adopted by other users; in the last phase of this sequence, the exchange of information between different users became saturated and only some messages reached potential new users, and for this reason the rate of spread of the new technique dropped. In the case of Bulliet's model, the flow of information about Islam would also be key to explaining the pattern of changes in conversion. However, Bulliet realized that, in order to complete the analogy, an explanation was needed to understand how potential converts could perceive the adoption of Islam as an improvement (*ibidem*: 26–32).

In wondering what allowed the success of Islam, Bulliet did not look for an explanation of the religion as inherently more or less attractive than other religions of the period. For him, the key was to define the conditions of the cultural milieu that could make conversion socially possible, acceptable or appealing to different individuals. Bulliet realized the difficulties inherent to the abandonment of a social identity, and he postulated that conversion to Islam would be produced almost exclusively within the conditions established by two axioms. The first axiom is that Islam should offer the new convert very similar conditions to those of the religion that they left behind. The second axiom is that the person that converts does not diminish significantly their social status under the new religion. These axioms, placed in the context where Bulliet was working, offered a quite detailed definition of the cultural milieu in which conversion could take place. Bulliet was looking mainly at Iran, and then to Iraq, Syria, Egypt, Tunisia and Iberia (al-Andalus), all places defined by the inheritance of late antique empires based on an urban civilization and complex and hierarchical religious structures. The implication of Bulliet's theory is that as Islam was spreading over these areas, it was being shaped by the new converts in a fashion that made it comparable to the older urban religions of the area, and so the first axiom of Bulliet was made possible. It is easy to follow up the same reasoning and end up realizing that the fulfilling of the second axiom is achieved with this process as well. The conversion of the urban population and the materialization of the first axiom led to the social structuration of the body of believers, therefore making it possible that more and more people could convert and yet keep their social status with little change (*ibidem*: 33–42).

There are a number of objections that can be made to Bulliet's model. The main one is that the model forces one to consider Islam as a simple technological idea that is transmitted in a pattern that we would define as viral today: as a zero-sum game in which the population is clearly separated into two categories: Muslims and those who are not yet Muslims. Islam, however, is a very complicated body of beliefs and practices, and its transmission involved a much more complex and protracted pattern of contacts between Muslims and non-Muslims (cf. Carlson 2015; Carvajal López 2013a; and the case of Eaton 1993, discussed below). Another problem is that Bulliet's model focuses on developments in urban contexts exclusively, leaving aside changes in the rural world. To be sure, the two axioms that he uses to ensure the validity of his model serve to disqualify any society that does not fit into the pattern of urban contexts characteristic of the late antique states. The extensive rural world and the communities where social identity is constituted with reference to a large kin group or a tribe are excluded. An example referred to by Bulliet himself is the case of Berbers and Turkish tribes, where conversion was a formal utterance delivered by the tribal chiefs that did not necessarily convey social change (1979: 33–4). He assumed that the only conversion relevant to social change, and therefore to his model, was individual conversion, and that would be produced mainly in the urban communities, which grew with the affluence of new people. For my part, I do not consider it a good idea to ignore the potential for change in the rural and tribal world of the Abode of Islam, where recent archaeological work has shown abundant cultural and social changes.[7] It is not difficult to imagine that parallel and different processes of Islamization took place in these areas, and that Bulliet's model would fail to account for them. This criticism does not limit the value of the model as an approximation to the rates of conversion of large parts of the population of the early Islamic-period world, particularly around the towns; moreover, the reasoning followed by Bulliet to establish his model contains remarkable observations that show much about how the process of conversion to Islam is more than a succession of individual stories, but is an important step in the creation of an Islamic society. However, Bulliet is ultimately focused on documenting these individual conversions, rather than in explaining what he understands as the process of Islamization.

Al-Andalus: The formation of the Islamic society

The second model of Islamization that I would like to discuss in this chapter is one that is prevalent in the debate about al-Andalus, Islamic Iberia. It is a model proposed by Manuel Acién, historian and archaeologist, in a number of works published during the 1990s.[8] The first important thing that must be understood about Acién's theory is that it is inserted in a very complex debate about the formation of the Islamic society of al-Andalus, in which he incorporated ideas extracted from the debate about the transition between Antiquity and the Middle Ages that was being developed at a European level in that period of time. As in the case of Bulliet's work, the word 'Islamization' is not prominently used in Acién's writing. However, Islamization has been discussed in the body of research on al-Andalus that has followed Acién's work (as explained in more detail below), and therefore the debate is very relevant for this chapter.

Before Acién's theory, scholars' models of the formation of Andalusi society were based on the theory of Pierre Guichard (1976), who established that the Muslim conquest of Iberia of 711–714 marked a rupture with the Roman and Visigothic past of the peninsula.[9] The conquest was immediately followed by the settlement of sizeable groups of Berbers and Arabs who were organized along the lines of a tribal society. The influence of these newly arrived groups was enough to change the social organization of Iberia from patronage-based to kin-based structures (simplified in Guichard's work as 'weak' and 'strong' societies, or as Western and Eastern respectively). The implications of Guichard's theory were followed by Miquel Barceló, who established the centrality of the tribal social structure in Andalusi society and the relative freedom of rural and urban communities that were taxed directly by the state and not subjected to lordships ('a society without lords') (Barceló 1986).[10] Under this model, the Umayyad state of Cordoba was considered an offspring of Islamic society that was essentially composed of peasant communities and towns living under their own regimes (Barceló 1997).

Acién had agreed and even contributed to the construction of the model of Islamic society above. However, in 1994, he questioned some of the basic assumptions of that model with the introduction of theoretical insights coming from the European debate of the transformation of the Mediterranean world between Antiquity and the Middle Ages, and more particularly, Chris Wickham's remarks about the transition between the ancient and the feudal mode of production (1984). Wickham believed that the difference between those was based on how surplus was extracted from producer communities; tax was the characteristic way of the tributary mode of production, and rent was that of feudalism. He then proposed that the two modes of production could co-exist in the same social formation, although one of them would always be predominant. Acién adopted this identification between a way of surplus-extraction and modes of production for al-Andalus. In his new theory, Acién identified a class of rural-based landlords living in the fringes of the Umayyad state of Cordoba, sustained by rent-paying communities that were not under the control of the state. The Umayyad state was instead funded by tax-paying peasants. Acién stated that the formation of al-Andalus was the history of the transition between the societies of the pre-Islamic and post-Roman period, based on rent-paying communities, to the Islamic-period Umayyad state of Cordoba, which he identified with the Islamic social formation of al-Andalus. By placing the state as the focus of the transformation of society, he was stepping away from Guichard's theory.

In the face of the criticism that Wickham's opposition between tax and rent raised in Marxist circles (cf. Haldon 1997), and of his own positions in the debate of al-Andalus, Acién offered a more nuanced view of the Islamic social formation. According to Acién, the Islamic social formation was characterized by four main features: the dominance of the urban over the rural world, the hegemony of the private over the public sphere, the adoption of a political philosophy based on the thought of Muslim philosophers and the association to specific forms of material culture. It is perhaps not surprising to see here a reflection of the same focus on urban contexts noted in Bulliet's model, but with an important difference: individual conversion is completely irrelevant for Acién's theory.

Already in the initial formulation of his theory in 1994, Acién noted that several examples of the communities that he classified as rent-paying, and therefore, feudal, were led by Muslim lords. He found no issue with that, because in his conception, the religion professed by the individuals was not relevant in the formation of the Islamic society of al-Andalus (or Islamization); in his theory, Islamization becomes identified with the formation of the Umayyad state and the social order associated to it. For Acién, therefore, Islamization is an issue of the hegemonic imposition of an Islamic elite with a very particular model of state, and conversion to Islam follows.

The theory of Acién forms the backbone of the most accepted view of Islamization in al-Andalus by archaeologists and historians. In particular, Sonia Gutiérrez Lloret has applied his theories of formation of the Islamic society in Tudmīr (East of Spain) (Gutiérrez Lloret 1996; 2007; 2012), and has generated a model of transition between the late antique and the Islamic period that has been adopted in the interpretation of archaeological data in many other areas of Iberia (e.g. Alba Calzado and Gutiérrez Lloret 2008; Amorós and Gutiérrez Lloret 2020; García 2019). Acién's model of development of the state and city has been defined in more detail by Eduardo Manzano Moreno (2006) and Eneko López Martínez de Marigorta (2020). However, Acién's ideas have also sparked acrimonious criticism. His focus on a top-to-bottom change was considered unjustified by Barceló, whose conception of al-Andalus foregrounded the transformations in peasants' communities before that of the Umayyad state (Barceló 1997). Some of Acién's interpretations of change in material culture have also been questioned and are in need of revision (e.g. Martínez Enamorado 2003: 534–53). Finally, Acién's consideration of the formation of the Islamic society as a process of transition between Antiquity and the Umayyad state overlooks the role of immigrant groups in al-Andalus, and alternative processes of Islamization that necessarily took part in the formation of the Umayyad society (Carvajal López 2019; 2022; forthcoming). As in the case of Bulliet, the criticism of Acién's model does not involve its total rejection. Its greatest virtue is to highlight the need to analyze how an Islamic society where conversion can become a reasonable option is established. However, the problem of this model is that its distance with the idea of conversion as a cause does not dispel the feeling that Islam appears as an ideological agglutinant for the Umayyad state of Cordoba. In other words, Acién rejects the idea of Islam as a force of change but considers it as a prescriptive moral code in support of the Umayyad state apparatus instead.

The concept of Islamicate culture: Beyond religion?

In slightly different ways, the two authors discussed above consider that Islamization requires a cultural superstructure that contributes to the shaping of the new Islamic society. Although Bulliet and Acién did not discuss this superstructure in detail, the concept can be put in relation to the idea of the Islamicate culture and its correlates, such as Islamdom, that were coined by Marshall Hodgson in his monumental *Venture of Islam* (1974). Hodgson used these terms as a way of addressing the culture of Islamic societies without necessarily involving religion (which would be correlated to words such as Islamic, Muslim and

Islam) (Hodgson 1974, Vol I: 57–60). In his definition, he stated that Islamicate was also a reference to the cultural milieu of the urban and cosmopolitan classes of Islamdom. Hodgson places a fundamental difference in the high culture of Islam (or Islamicate, as he would define it), which was shared across the Islamic world (or Islamdom), and the popular culture of particular spaces under Islamic domination, which should be understood in regional or local terms (*ibidem*: 91–2).

The work of Hodgson has had much echo in recent historical studies, where the term Islamicate has become commonplace. In his revision of the concept, Shahab Ahmed has praised Hodgson's remarkable attempt to bring clarity into the field of Islamic studies with his powerful vision but has also noted that very often the term Islamicate is adopted more out of a shortage of interpretations than because of a theoretical awareness of its advantages and drawbacks (2016: 158). The main problem that Ahmed points out is that an essential flaw in Hodgson's careful intellectual building becomes magnified in the 'sliding scale' of his followers' interpretations. This flaw consists in Hodgson's pietist conception of Islam as a religion, which establishes a lineal, single-dimensional progression between a religious core (Islam) and its cultural derivation (Islamicate). This schema has the virtue of safeguarding the numinous aspects of the faith of Islam, placing them at the heart of what Muslims do, rather than aside. However, it also puts Islamic religion in a position to prescribe behaviour that becomes too easily magnified into a normative conception of Islam (*ibidem*: 157–71). The distinction between Islamic and Islamicate serves also to establish a centrality of some aspects and versions of Islam over others. In a comment about a work of Bruce Lawrence about Islamicate civilization in Asia, Ahmed notes that 'the pre-categorization of Islam as *religion* – and thus as belief, ritual, doctrine, law and *sameness*– is accepted without demur; anything beyond this, anything that exceeds this – that is, *history* and *society*, *ethics* and *difference* – is Islamicate' (*ibidem*: 172; Italics in the original text). In this range of variety and difference that Ahmed is trying to salvage from Hodgson's pietist excess, are the manifestations that non-Muslims play a role within Islamic culture and history. For example, the

Jewish intellectual Mūsā b. Maymūn / Maimonides (1138–1204 CE) would be considered Islamicate in Hodgson's conception, but Ahmed considers his endeavour absolutely in line with the framework of Islamic philosophy, *kalām*-theology and *fiqh*-jurisprudence of his time and thus fully Islamic despite his Jewish faith (*ibidem*: 174–5).

The relevance of Ahmed's criticism of Hodgson's Islamicate concept is that it has application to similar works that try to steer away from the numinous aspects of religion when analyzing Islamization, such as the examples of Bulliet and Acién highlighted above. The sliding scale described above means that the attempt to escape the impossibility to grasp individual conversion can all too easily be translated into a prescriptive and normative conception of religious identity, whether under the supervision of specialist scholars or of an interventionist state. Ahmed locates the essence of the problem in the Quaker (Christian) roots of Hodgson's thought, which led to his assumption that Islam and Christianity are 'mutually intelligible', and in particular that the separation between 'religious' and 'non-religious' spheres can be made to work in parallel. Ahmed, based on his knowledge of literary expressions of Muslims in what he calls the Balkan-to-Bengal complex in the last thousand years, begs to differ. He does not believe that the division of religious/non-religious can work in pre-modern Islam in the same way as in Christianity, because the '*scale* and *normativity*' of the '*con-founding*' and '*con-fusion*' among the two spheres in Islam is not 'conceptually and analytically commensurable' (*ibidem*: 166; all Italics are in the original). Ahmed is here expressing in his own terms the criticism that Asad raised to anthropological abuses on Islam (see Chapter 1) but is also making another extremely relevant point: the uniqueness of Islam does not lie only in its conception of the numinous. On the contrary, a part of what makes Islam unique emerges out of its own trajectory of the history of engagement of Muslims (and non-Muslims) with Islam. This means that an analysis of Islamic societies, and of Islamization, cannot expect to become more precise simply by isolating the numinous aspects of the religion to a particular sphere beyond rational explanation.

Return to religion in Islamization: Conversion and cultural change

In the pages above, the problems associated with a conception of Islamization based only on conversion to Islam have been highlighted. However, any attempt to dispose of the idea of conversion in Islamization is also problematic, because it leads inevitably to a separation between the religious and the secular spheres that is incommensurable with pre-modern Islam. In the pages that follow I will analyze some approaches that have considered religion and society at the same time when discussing Islamization.

East Bengal: Islam as a transformative religion

The first case study of this section is Eaton's, already mentioned above. He is concerned with the context and explanation of the Islamization of East Bengal (1993), one of the most densely populated Muslim areas in the Indian subcontinent. To understand this phenomenon, he develops a nuanced and well-informed historical approach that takes him beyond the limits of the general models described above. For Eaton, it is essential to link the success of mass conversion to the configuration of Islam as a transformative ideology of the world.

The area of East Bengal, the frontier of the Mughal area of influence, was colonized from at least the sixteenth century. This process of colonization was driven by pioneers who combined organizational skills and charisma to be able to attract and mobilize communities to settle in the lands, regardless of their religious beliefs. These communities were locals, but also migrants from other areas of Bengal and even from India. Although the activities related to land clearance and cultivation are the main explanation why these pioneers were most venerated and remembered, most of them were also Muslims who obtained land grants by the Mughal rulers and who founded mosques and shrines in the newly colonized territories. The environmental and social changes produced by this process of colonization were slow but extraordinary in the long term, and marked the development of post-sixteenth century Bengali society. During this process, Islam came to be understood as a transformative ideology associated with settling the land and expanding agriculture. At the same time, a sizeable demographic growth increased the rural mass established in the new lands opened by a charismatic Muslim gentry supported by the Mughal administration. Other religious communities existed, but they were minor in numbers and had less state support, and therefore their outreach was more limited (*ibidem*: 194–267).

Between the seventeenth and the twentieth centuries there was a process of conversion of the rural masses in close contact with this religious gentry. This process was protracted and fluid, and it should be understood as linked to a progressive social change produced by the environmental and economic transformations that were taking place in the frontier region, rather than as a process in which people were convinced to abandon a religion in acceptance of another. The analysis that Eaton makes of this process is based on the observation of the material culture and, especially, literature of the area and period under study. The process can be heuristically organized in three phases (although Eaton warns that the reality was fluid and not easily framed in this scheme). The first one was a stage of coexistence, the phase where those under the conversion process came to accept the display of Islamic narratives of supernatural agency along their own local beliefs; there was no process of selection or even comparison between traditions, as the different elements were not presented in a way that the elimination of the other was required, and the Bengali rural communities that Eaton targeted seemed to have been open to these changes. The phase of identification was the next step, and it represented the stage in which the converts made an explicit identification between the supernatural forces of the Islamic tradition and those of their local traditions. And finally, displacement was the phase in which pre-Islamic supernatural agencies were discarded in the benefit of Islamic ones (*ibidem*: 268–303). Islamic beliefs also permeated other levels of social practice during this period of conversion. Although shrines, mosques and Islamic schools became more abundant in the landscape, the association of religion with literacy and the gender division of work expanded progressively, making Eastern Bengali society distinctly different to its Western counterpart by the twentieth century. However, the Islamic society of East Bengal was also characteristic in its own right, because of the mixing of traditions. As an example, Eaton cites the use of Quranic texts in magical (not religious) rituals still in the late-nineteenth and twentieth centuries (*ibidem*: 294–7) and an eighteenth-century poem portraying women and men working the fields together, something that was unthinkable in the more rigid Islamic society of the twentieth century (*ibidem*: 299–301).

With this work, Eaton achieves a well contextualized and fine-grained analysis of the process of Islamization in East Bengal. The process fits well within the very specific conditions of the colonization of the frontier lands of the Mughal Empire in Bengal and the configuration of Islam as a religion specifically supportive of the process of land clearance and expansion of cultivation. The concession of lands by the Mughals and the creation of a Muslim gentry who allowed the settlement of local communities facilitated sustained contacts between Islamic and native beliefs, and eventually the adoption of Islam by the masses and the different belief systems merged. The process of Islamization was ultimately a process of generation of a new Islamic community with a particular way of understanding Islam. The main question that this analysis raises is how far it can be applied to other contexts, given its highly specific contextual implications.

The Islamization of Sub-Saharan Africa: Considering multiple paths

Eaton's study of the Islamization of Eastern Bengal, and in particular his phased approach, has influenced the approach of the archaeologist who has probably dedicated more pages to Islamization in the past few years: Tim Insoll. Insoll's interests encompass global Islam, but it is mainly in his background as an Africanist where the main inspiration of his original approaches to Islamization can be found. Religious change in African contexts – including conversion to Islam – had been analyzed by anthropologists, historians and archaeologists (e.g. Fisher 1973; 1985; Horton 1971; 1975; 1993; Thorold 1987; Trimingham 1968). Already in his 1996 analysis of the Islamization of Gao (Mali), Insoll challenged the traditional assumption of forcible conversion by the Almohads in Western Africa (e.g. Levtzion 1973) and proposed an explanation of Islamization developed along a three-part scheme – quarantine, mixing and reform – [11] based on the phases of staged conversion developed by Fisher (1985) and used by Thorold (1987). The similarities with Eaton's model are evident, and although Insoll's conclusions were based on the Africanists' experience, his analysis is as fine-grained and concerned with social and cultural change in relation to conversion as that of Eaton in East Bengal. Insoll analyzed the appeal of Islam in the different social groups of Gao: urban dwellers, nomads and sedentary agriculturalists, and its impact in the political and belief structures. He noted the development of an Islam well adapted to the African society where it was established, a concept that he developed afterwards in his classic *Archaeology of Islam*: an Islamization adapted to local circumstances (1999: 9–11) that inspired similar views in other scholars (e.g. Carvajal López 2013a; Inskip 2013a; 2013b; Lape 2000).

In later approaches to the Islamization of different regions of Sub-Saharan Africa, Insoll has applied Eaton's three-phased scheme of coexistence, identification and displacement, because he believes that it allows for a better characterization of 'gradual religious change and, importantly, assimilation of older elements within the process as well' (Insoll 2003: 29; 2016: 247). In his most recent work, he has engaged with the archaeology of Islam of different areas of Sub-Saharan Africa (e.g. Insoll 2003; 2016; 2017; 2020; Insoll et al 2021b) and of the Persian Gulf (e.g. Insoll 2005; Insoll et al 2021a). His interpretations are historically well-contextualized narratives of conversion understood in the context of change in a multitude of dimensions that may include different stages of trade, warfare and ideological exchange, technological and environmental innovations, and the development of new social and political structures. This detailed approach allows for differences in the process of Islamization to emerge in each area. For example, despite the similarity of religious practices and the relevance of trade in the Western Sahel and the Horn of Africa, the evidence points to a more protracted conversion in the former than in the latter. The nomads, exposed to trade with the Muslims, seem to have been much more influential in the initial spread of Islam in Western Sahel, whereas the towns of Ethiopia, and in particular Harar and Harlaa, were the main foci of spread of Islam. Even when the role of towns as centres of diffusion of Islam is compared, differences emerge. The role of saints is fundamental in Harar, whereas it is more reduced and constrained in time in the centres of the Sahel such as Gao or Timbuktu (Insoll 2016; 2017).

As in the case of Eaton, Insoll's analysis of Islamization in its different contexts has much to praise, as they achieve an integration of conversion as a reasonable option embedded in a complex network of cultural and social transformations. However, a question emerges. If Islamization cannot be conceived of as one single process, but as different ones adapted to particular contexts, how can we consider that the result of the different Islamizations is the same Islam? Are we talking about different versions of Islam or even of different Islams?

One or many Islamizations?

The question of whether there is one Islam or more than one is indeed quite old in the anthropology of Islam, and we have seen it briefly in Chapter 1. Insoll himself considered it in his 1999 work, and his answer was to conceive Islam as a superstructure shaping different local instances. The problem with this perspective, as I have noted above, is that it assumes an implicit separation between Islam and society. Society changes at its own pace, in its own historical time, while Islam remains somehow external (though not necessarily reified, as in previous anthropological representations) and within a different historical line that allows Muslims from contexts as diverse as Gao, Harar, Bahrein or

Bengal to be aware of their own (structural) commonalities beyond their differences. This perspective avoids some of the major pitfalls of the two extremes of the Islam *vs* Islams debate, which have been well analyzed by Ahmed (2016: 129–52). However, it also incurs in the problem of identifying Islam 'in terms of a fundamental corpus of creed and practice' (Ahmed 2016: 140; cf. Insoll 1999: 1), which leads to the misleading impression that Muslims are connected simply by their agreement in the acceptance of such content. Ahmed believes that the power of Islam to connect Muslims is based not on agreement, but on intelligibility. In other words, Islam 'furnishes the ground for *mutual existential intelligibility and sympathy,* – that is, for *shared inter-personal meaning*'. This shared meaning allows for an intimacy and identification that makes possible 'an encounter whereby the Self is transported, transposed to and seen in another person who [...] would, *in terms other than Islam / the Islamic*, be the Other, but who, in the experience of Islam, becomes one with the Self' (Ahmed 2016: 142; Italics in the original).

Setting the question of Islamization in Ahmed's terms, therefore, requires not only embedding conversion in cultural change (a task admirably performed by Eaton and Insoll), but also charting how, along that change, Islam becomes a ground for cultural intelligibility and intimacy. This perspective has the additional virtue of overcoming the identification between Islamization and conversion, because the former is not limited to documenting the adherence of new converts to Islam (in whatever way we may conceive it). Islamization is not a process that begins without Islam and ends in an Islamic society; it is rather a process of generating particular ways of becoming human in an Islamic context, independently of the point of departure and of the point of arrival. To understand Ahmed requires studying Islam from the perspective of meaning and feeling. In the next chapter I will explore the relationship between Islam, feeling and meaning, and how that can contribute to our study of Islamization.

3

Islamic Identity and *Being Islamic*

In the previous chapter I explained that Islamization should be considered not only from the perspective of religious conversion, but as the cultural change that makes that conversion possible. It is also important not to lose perspective on the inappropriateness of the separation between religious and secular spheres when looking at pre-modern Islam, something that is counterintuitive to academic observers today. This requires us to think about Islamization as the cultural change that allows the generation of particular meanings and feelings that are proper of an Islamic context (and Con-Text, following Shahab Ahmed). Islamization does not necessarily start and end with conversion.

In consonance with this programme, in this chapter I will search to understand feeling and meaning in Islam. The first approach to this field requires us to think about the Islamic Self (according to Ahmed) or the Islamic identity, according to Gabrielle Marranci whose works I comment on below.

Islamic identities: From norm to feeling

We have seen how difficult it is to address the idea of identity from the point of view of a cause. To ask someone why they have an identity (*why they are something*) is very likely to return a self-referential or a self-affirmative answer and is not very useful to understand the identity in itself. A similar problem appears when trying to analyze an identity from a normative perspective, that is, as defined by the acceptance of a set of rituals and practices. In the case of Muslim identity, these rituals and practices can be very different from one branch of Islam to the next, but also at the level of individuals. In the same way, I hold, following Ahmed, that it is not possible to isolate an identity only in terms of belief, at least if that belief is defined as the discursive acceptance of a set of doctrines and practices. From this point of view, militant belief in a dogma is not very different from other rituals and practices in a formalist consideration of an identity. Dogmata, principles, rituals or practices can be used for establishing *doxa*, orthodoxy within social organizations as defined from the point of view of an identity, but they are still no more than rules that someone needs to accept to become an approved member of those organizations. However, it is beyond the power of social organizations to control individual identities *as they are felt*.

In the particular case of Muslims, this is the concept of faith explained in Chapter 1, a basic positioning with respect to a 'great drama of decision' as conceptualized by Wilfred Cantwell Smith (1981: 122). If one tries to look at Muslim identity from a historical point of view instead, the result is a wide range of different branches of Muslims with different perspectives about orthodoxy. In fact, it is not possible to define the limits of the overall community of Muslims, the *umma*, because not all those who affirm to be members are recognized as such by other members (this is what Gabrielle Marranci has called the '*umma* paradox': 2008: 101–15). This should hardly be surprising. The long and eventful Islamic history is full of divisions, splits and competition between different branches and sects on account of particular historical events and the interpretation of their meaning for Islam. As time went on, different dogmatic paths were created and each one of them was supported by sizeable groups of believers. The dogmata of some branches can be considered as outside of the orthodoxy of the *umma* by scholars of a rival branch.

Islamic identity has been the focus of the works of Gabrielle Marranci (2006; 2008). He has developed an anthropological approach to the concept of identity (2006: 31–52; 2008: 89–102) that will be presented in what needs to be a simplified version for reasons of space.

Marranci departs from an exploration of the generic concept of identity in anthropology, observing that in the twentieth century it has been based on perspectives from psychology and sociology that emphasized social constructivist conceptualizations. These theories have an impact on the concept of individuality itself. To a large extent, the role of the individual became much less relevant in social models where culture was a powerful force in shaping identities. Identities would be a sort of empty social role where individuals would fit themselves, changing identities as they went through life. In other words, the agency of individuals was rarely present in the mechanisms of identity formation, and when it was, it presented individuals driven by self-interested calculations to adapt themselves to – that is, to 'perform' – pre-conceived notions of identity hold by mechanisms of group pressure in their cultural context (in a way not far removed from the idea of normative identities). Marranci criticizes the idea that individuals are forced to 'perform' these identities, and therefore they are not being what they feel they ought to be (2006: 40). For him, this is a key point: 'I am what I feel to be' is nothing less that the title of his Chapter 3 (*ibidem*: 31–52). Muslim identity therefore consists in 'feeling to be a Muslim', that is, having a particular emotional response to Islam.

Analyzing Muslim identity from this perspective requires a concept of the individual as a stable but active entity, capable of producing and manifesting emotions. To ground this concept, Marranci uses Antonio Damasio's neurological studies about feeling and emotion (2000). From an eminently evolutionary perspective, Damasio conceives feeling and emotion as two different things. Emotions are bodily responses to external stimuli, from changes in heart rate to facial expressions. Feelings, however, are mental expressions of such bodily states that leave a lasting mark in the memory, and therefore in the conscience, of the individual mind. In his studies on the brain, Damasio found out that there are different levels of the self where the impact of emotions and feelings are distinct. At the most basic level there is what Damasio calls 'proto-self' (*ibidem*: 22), consisting of a neural map of the body and a basic awareness of its state with respect to environmental conditions. This proto-self is present in all living beings, from monocellular paramecia and all the way up in the evolutionary chain. It simply serves the purpose of 'alerting' the body to take actions to react to environmental changes that may be dangerous. In complex organisms, however, there are more elaborate systems of self that give rise to consciousness. In the human mind there are at least two levels, the core consciousness, related to the core self, and the extended consciousness, related to the autobiographical self. The core consciousness is generated by the mechanism of the core self, which is constantly monitoring changes in the proto-self, and gives the mind the feeling of knowing, that is, the awareness of self-conscience (*ibidem*: 82-106). The extended consciousness is formed when the core self relates this awareness to the memories of previous states of the self (which Damasio calls 'autobiographical memories'), by means of the autobiographical self (*ibidem*: 17-18). The extended consciousness is therefore the sense of being a single entity that belongs to a temporal line with a past, a future and a historical continuity (*ibidem*: 195-233). Emotions, as bodily states, and feelings, as mental representations of emotions, are essential for the formation of the different levels of the self and of the consciousness, as are the autobiographical memories of the feelings that different states of the core self produces, which are stored in the mind. With all this, human beings can recognize their own individuality as the result of a 'delicately shaped selectional machinery of our imagination [which] stakes the probabilities of selection [of experiences] towards the same, historically continuous self' (*ibidem*: 225, in Marranci 2006: 47). The individual is therefore understood as a changing entity over a stable base, the continuous self, built on continuous reference to an autobiographical memory.

With such a definition of an individual, Marranci goes on to define identity. For him, this identity has two parts: a) it is a mental arrangement that allows us to make sense of the autobiographical self and b) it makes possible to communicate that self through symbols (2006: 47; 2008: 97). I will leave the discussion of the second part of the definition for later in the text. As for the first part of the definition, it means that identity is intrinsic to the development of individuality; that is, far from having an origin in a normative rule of the group, identities are felt through emotions (first) and feelings (second). In essence, identities are specific constructions of the imagination making sense of the autobiographical self through a tautological circuit in which human beings live. The tautological circuit is a chain of events in the individual mind that are set in motion when a stimulus generated in the environment of the self (stage 1) sets in motion an emotional response (stage 2), which is then translated in a feeling, a mental representation (stage 3). The feeling then affects the autobiographical self (stage 4), and this is interpreted through the mental arrangement that forms the identity (stage 5) and the identity itself is affected by the feeling (stage 6) (Marranci 2008: 97–8). The tautological circuit, in short, produces a re-evaluation of the identity with respect to a new relationship between the internal milieu of the individual and its external environment. A stable identity is maintained as long as there is a balanced connection between those two parts. If the re-evaluation of the new situation at the end of the tautological circuit is unbalanced, then a crisis of identity is produced and the individual feels that there is a danger of schismogenesis, that is, of a 'tendency of individuals to move apart through a systematic and divergent interaction produced by negative feedback' (Marranci 2006: 11).[1] When this situation occurs, an act of identity is required as a symbol (*ibidem*: 47) to reaffirm the identity under threat and to move towards a re-establishment of the balance between individual identity and environment.

This leads us to the second part of the definition of identities. They allow the communication of the self though symbols. Marranci's take on symbols is different from the most accepted definition of the concept in anthropology, that of Clifford Geertz (1973), which establishes that symbols are extrinsic sources of information and are therefore external to individuals (Marranci 2006: 47–8). Marranci thinks instead that symbols need to be part of the mechanism that allows identities to be felt, i.e. the tautological circuit. Thus, he prefers Victor Turner's definition of symbols as elements that do not only carry information, but that have the potential to produce changes in human behaviour (Turner 1967, in Marranci 2006: 48) by 'rousing, channelling and domesticating powerful emotions' (Turner 1969: 42–3, in Marranci 2006: 48). Acts of identity, the response to the danger of schismogenesis in the tautological circle, are symbols designed to correct unbalances in identity, to make them relevant to the task of making sense to the autobiographical self again (Marranci 2006: 50).

Symbols for Marranci are key to introducing archaeology in this question. In semiotics, a symbol is a sign with a link between a signifier and a signified that is culturally built. This makes it possible, to a certain extent, to reconcile Geertz's and Marranci's conceptions of the symbol as something that is at the same time outside the mind and a part of the tautological circuit. The signifier is external to the mind of the individual, while the signified is formed inside. In other words, the signifier is a particular stimulus of the environment that produces particular emotions and feelings, while the signified is built in the mind of the individual making sense of these emotions and feelings by linking them to particular bits of information of the autobiographical memory. Now, this requires us to accept that the link between signifier and signified is not built culturally, as in the classical conception of symbol, but through the continuum represented by the tautological circuit. Symbols then can be conceptualized as concepts or schemas, but they are special in the sense that the link between their material signifier and their mental signified are linked with a specific reference to the identity that is represented by the symbol.

It is worth returning briefly to the case of Islam in this thread to contemplate with precise examples what Marranci means with the danger of schismogenesis and acts of identity. A process of schismogenesis is unleashed by an event that threatens the dissolution or annihilation of the group to which the individual belongs by virtue of their identity. This danger does not need to be real; it just needs to be perceived as such. Marranci uses this concept in his 2006 work to create a framework to understand the extreme acts of terror that could be done by jihadists, that is, people who have been made to believe that the whole *umma* is in danger because of the current climate of aggressions towards Muslims. The schismogenesis here was identified with the disappearance of

Muslims and Islam altogether, and the act of identity that is required is a supreme sacrifice that reinstates the strength of Muslim identity. However, Marranci recognizes that there are many other perceptions of schismogenesis and strategies to devise acts of identity (2008: 98). I would like to refer to particular brave acts of social justice, kindness and forgiveness that are offered by many Muslims in the face of external aggression. A good example is the reaction of Mohammed Mahmoud, the imam of the Finsbury Park Mosque (London), after the terrorist attack that left one person dead and ten injured on 19 June 2017. Mahmoud personally protected the terrorist from physical attacks by a group of people who had restrained him until the police arrived. When he was later hailed as a hero by the media, he declared that his actions were the norm, not the exception, for Muslims. In this case, the schismogenesis that Mahmoud feared was not a literal annihilation of the Muslim community, but a misidentification of Muslims as violent people produced by the all too abundant misrepresentation in the media. His act of identity highlights the values of peace, justice and respect for the law that are distinctive on his take on Islamic doctrine, and in a more local context he also underlined British Muslims as part of the mosaic of identities that compose the modern city of London (Wazir 2017).[2]

I return now to the general argument on identity. The emotional feedback necessary for the tautological circuit, as well as the perception of danger of schismogenesis and the need for acts of identity, serve to consider the external influences in the formation of identity, that is, the part that is generated outside the individual mind. It is important to note here that this external world is still far wider than the social world. In fact, Marranci conceptualizes this part using Kay Milton's suggestion that 'emotions are an ecological rather than a social phenomenon, that they are a mechanism through which an individual human being is connected to and learns from the environment' (Milton 2005: 32 in Marranci 2006: 44). The main problem that an archaeologist finds in Marranci's theories is the passive role of the environment, of culture, in the shaping of individuals and identities beyond the generation of stimuli; all the important processes occur inside the mind of the individual, even the determination of symbols. Marranci seems to have gone too far in his escape from social determinism and has reached an essentially idealist conception of the individual, where all social and cultural aspects are mental reflections of what otherwise seem to be a pool of unorganized external stimuli.

Marranci's is not the only attempt in anthropological theory to offer a conciliatory approach to the division between individual and culture. A more fluid attempt is the work of Maurice Bloch, *Anthropology and the Cognitive Challenge* (2012), where he suggests that the concept of the individual is a meta-representation of what he calls the 'blob'. The blob is a biological phenomenon with a neurological system that gives it different levels of consciousness and autobiographical memory. The different levels of consciousness of the blob do not end with the biological individual itself; on the contrary, the blob's consciousness becomes seamlessly entangled with those of other blobs, in a process in which 'the blob is not just situated [...]; it is in itself moulded and modified by it to a significant degree' (*ibidem*: 139). This continuity of consciousness also reaches to the environment, by means of what Bloch terms 'concepts' and 'schemata', that is, mental phenomena activated by the 'co-ocurrence of the mental process and the social process' (*ibidem*: 163–4).

It is relevant to look at Bloch's work here to illustrate the weakest point of Marranci's elaborate argument: the need for a stable concept of individual. Bloch shows how this concept needs to be transformed in a meta-representation in order to make the most of the evolutionary ideas brought about by neuroscience in the cognition debate, and thus Marranci's concept of identity becomes compromised. Another aspect that is worth highlighting is the absolute disconnection of Islamic belief from Marranci's argument. He has enshrined the concept of belief under the guise of an Islamic individual identity that remains opaque. What Hodgson or Acién had done by separating religion and society, Marranci has re-enacted by keeping identity and belief apart. Interesting, as the mental dynamics that he describes can be used indistinctly to describe any kind of identity, Islamic or not. At the end of the argument, even if Marranci argues for a connection between the mind and the world, Islam cannot be found in the mind of the Muslims, so we must search for it in the external stimuli.

A different path: From feeling to hermeneutics

The problem of humanness

Marranci attempts to escape the limitation of a normativist approach to the Islamic identity by focusing on the feeling of being Muslim (or Islamic), that is, on the feelings produced by identification with the Islamic community. For Marranci, Islam is ultimately a map of discourses and interpretations about the feeling of being a Muslim (2008: 13–30), and therefore depends ultimately on a feeling that is generated and interpreted in the mind of the individual and shared through symbols. This approach requires the acceptance of the idea of symbols to establish a link between the mind of the person and the environment. As a result, the position of Islam remains unclear. It cannot take shape only in the chaos of external stimuli of the material world, but it is not in the mind of individuals either, as the mental mechanisms that Marranci develops could be used to explain any identity.

The theory of Marranci is very clear on the fact that Islam does not exist beyond the minds of Muslims. All the material manifestations of Islam are simply stimuli for Muslims, and it is not possible for non-Muslims to interpret them. Following this, a non-Muslim (like myself) should find that Islam is in itself inaccessible. Even though I can learn to understand the signs that Muslims use to express their belief and feelings, and I can even feel empathy towards them in their moments of joy, fury and sorrow *as Muslims*, I am definitely locked away to Islam. Islam is simply *not there*.

And yet, how can Islam take shape in the minds of Muslims if they simply react to environmental stimuli? How can the minds of Muslims create and communicate all the rich variety and complexity of symbols and meanings associated to them if these are not inside them, and yet these minds are *no different* from any other non-Muslim human mind?

This problem can be addressed in a completely new light when considered from the perspective proposed by Ahmed to dispel the notion of normativity underpinning most modern academic conceptions of Islam. I have cited Ahmed repeatedly above, because his criticism of the separation of religion as a different sphere of society is most effective when considering perspectives held in anthropology, history and the archaeology of Islam (see Chapters 1 and 2). However, Ahmed's work is not limited to this criticism, and offers an original concept of Islam that is relevant to the questions that I am considering here. He suggests that Islam needs to be considered in relation to the hermeneutic (or exploratory) engagement of Muslims with the Revelation of God to the Prophet Muḥammad. Under this perspective, Islam is at the same time a medium and the result (the Con-Text) of the search for the Revelation of Muslims in the Text and in the Pre-Text (see Ahmed 2016: 343–68; also, Chapter 1). Ahmed's theory, therefore, allocates a generative power in Islam that Marranci's theory is missing. He overcomes the distinction between individual mind and environment with his idea of Con-Text, which is at the same time environment, symbol and part of the generative individual mind (medium and result). There is nothing evolutionary in Ahmed's theory, but paradoxically his vision is closer to that of Bloch, whose perspective blurs the boundary between individual mind and society (but maintains a solid dualism between mind and matter). The main difference between Ahmed's and Bloch's perspectives is the essence of humanity that they aspire to reach. Bloch's (and Marranci's) idea of humanity is based on evolutionary biology (and this explains his ultimate dualism). The concept of Islamic humanity that Ahmed proposes, however, is shaped by the search for the Revelation in the world.

Marranci's and Bloch's conception of humanity rests firmly on the type of Cartesian dualism that became the paradigm of Western modernity and is analyzed by Bruno Latour (1993) [1991]. In a way, both anthropologists are trying to find a way to bridge the separation between nature and culture, which is the same object of critique of the philosopher. But Latour goes beyond this, and with his analysis of purification, questions also the separation between subject and object that is still the foundation of the thinking of Marranci and Bloch. This can be noted in the conception of a stable individual of the former, and in the firm biological basis of the 'blob' in the latter.

There is a rich multidisciplinary literature following Latour's criticism of modernity, to which I return in the next chapter. I will just note here that the work of Latour opened the path to think about humans not as a pure result of biological evolution, and therefore as somehow apart from nature. The idea of humanness, of a human condition that is shaped in historical circumstances, has been suggested by John Barrett, despite his rejection of part of the critique of Latour to modernism (2014). More in line with the philosopher, archaeologists have learnt from other cultural approaches to personhood, identity and the human body (e.g. Fowler 2004; Robb and Harris 2013) to question the isolated and unchangeable essence of humanity. This has led to posthumanist and postanthropocentric approaches (Crellin 2020: 157–61; Harris 2021: 19–41), with implications relevant for this book, and which will be described in Chapter 4.

It is worth noting that Shahab Ahmed seems to reach a similar point about the fluidity of the human condition with his critique of the separation between the religious and the secular spheres. Ahmed's thoughts are focused on his criticism of the Victorian concept of religion, continuing Asad's anthropological critique (1993; 2009). And yet, as a believer, Ahmed endorses the conclusion of Wilfred Cantwell Smith: 'It is a mistake to think of the Islamic as one way of being religious. Rather, for fourteen centuries the Islamic has been one of the salient ways of being human' (1981: 12; in Ahmed 2016: 176). This Islamic conception of humanity, or humanness, is marked by the search for knowledge about the Revelation, so that 'the distinguishing human quality is knowledge' (Ahmed 2016: 376, on reading al-Fārābī's *The Excellent City*). The implication of this ideal of humanity is that all its dimensions are crucially constituted and oriented in terms of a spatial differentiation of Islamic Truth and Meaning developed across two axes: one of *hierarchy* and another one of *interiority / exteriority*. Ahmed illustrates this with an explanation of different levels of Truth and Meaning in cosmology (higher / Unseen/ unrevealed vs lower /Seen / revealed) and in society (where there is a hierarchy of 'more- and less-Truth-proficient souls', separated by 'the capacity to know Truth' (*ibidem*: 367–8).³ In this way, although Ahmed does not question modernity in the way that Latour and his followers have, he does highlight the historicity of the human condition and its intimate relationship with the world beyond the individual.

A hermeneutical approach

For the purposes of this book, Ahmed's *Being Islamic* therefore offers two precious advantages over Marranci's theory. One is that it is a theory based on exploration of the meaning of the Revelation as the origin of mutual intelligibility, and therefore it is better suited to explain Islam and Islamization than a theory based on the mind-body dualism. The other one is that the idea of Con-Text speaks of the co-determination of Islam and Islamic (human) beings, and therefore dispels the need to establish a stable self (Marranci) or a biological base (Bloch) to which an external, material environment needs to be opposed. That makes Ahmed's theory very useful for archaeologists, despite the fact that the author discusses Islamic archaeology very superficially.⁴

For Ahmed, the Islamic human being is defined by their capacity to learn knowledge about the Revelation, that is, about Islamic Truth and Meaning. That knowledge, or meaning, is present in the world, because 'Islam *precedes* the Muslim' (Ahmed 2016: 362; Italics in the original), even if the Muslim goes on to produce new meaning. The key to the link between Islamic meaning and humans (or Muslims) is his concept of Con-Text, which has been defined in Chapter 1 (see also above). To be sure, Con-Text is the assemblage of meanings of Revelation that have been produced in past human and historical engagements with

Islam and that are present as Islam in a historical context (*ibidem*: 356). It is important to note that Ahmed makes a difference between Con-Text *in toto*, that is, the totality of meanings of Revelation in a historical period, and Con-Text *in loco*, or the set of Con-Textual meanings available in a particular historical context (*ibidem*: 361). But there is a second dimension of Con-Text to consider: by the same definition provided above, it is also the result of the hermeneutical engagement of Muslims with the Revelation. The question to consider, therefore, is how elements of a historical context become Islamic Con-Text.

Ahmed provides in his work some examples of elements or fields that in principle are not directly related to Islam and can become the locus of Con-Text, that is, they can acquire Islamic meaning. This meaning can be found or generated beyond the content of the Quran and the Hadith (Text), in what Ahmed call Pre-Text, involving all the aspects of the world that pre-exist the Textual form of the Revelation. He provides examples in art (*ibidem*: 408–25), science (*ibidem*: 430–5), music (425–30), rulership (*ibidem*: 453–82) and even violence (*ibidem*: 452). Islamic meaning can also be made from explicitly non-Muslim cultural products, such as pre-Islamic philosophy and myths (*ibidem*: 435–44) or aspects of Javanese paganism (*ibidem*: 450–2). Crucially for archaeologists, he includes historical examples of material culture: wine consumption (*ibidem*: 57–73), wearing hats in crooked ways (*ibidem*: 202–6) and figural arts (*ibidem*: 415–26). Muslims will read and produce Con-Text in different ways, all of them meaningful and mutually intelligible, but also diverse and even contradictory. The generation of Islamic meaning is contingent, and therefore it will be read in different ways by people with different relationships to the material culture, and this is what allows them to disagree meaningfully within Islam.

But Muslims are not the only ones that can engage in Con-Text. Islamic meaning is something that can be appreciated and generated by non-Muslims actively engaging with Con-Text, such as Sikh wrestlers shouting 'Yā 'Alī!' to go to combat; Vijayanagari courtiers adopting Islamic garments and protocols; or Jewish scholars using the argumentation of Islamic *kalām* (theology) (*ibidem*: 444–9). It is 'the commitment of the self to the making of meaning in terms of the hermeneutical engagement with the Revelation of Islam* that makes the action of the non-Muslim *Islamic*' (*ibidem*: 446, Italics in the original).

That does not mean that the same signifier, or element of context, cannot be meaningful beyond the Islamic Con-Text. 'The act is one, but the categorical meanings of the act are more than one' (*ibidem*: 446). To make this case, Ahmed presents some examples of non-Muslims who engage with Con-Textual vocabulary and forms without making meaning for their own self: a non-Muslim architect building a mosque, the makers of porcelain wine-bowls produced in China to export all over the Islamic world and non-Muslim scholars of Islamic studies. Ahmed here distinguishes between the producer (non-Islamic) and the product (Islamic) (*ibidem*: 449–50). The product of the work is Islamic because it contains the vocabulary and forms to make it meaningful for those who are actively engaged in the search for the meaning of the Revelation, even if the producer is not. As I will explain in Chapters 4 and 6, my answer in this case is that the architect, the potters and the scholars *become* Islamic as a consequence of their engagement with Con-Text.

In summary, we can say that Islamization results with the exploration of a given historical context in light of the Con-Text *in loco* and brings about the creation or renovation of Con-Text for Muslims, and the adoption of Con-Textual meaning by non-Muslims. Beyond the creation of Con-Text, Islamization is a historical process with an uncertain result from its point of departure: it is not possible to determine which type of society it will produce. We may even question that the result of Islamization is an Islamic society, since the Islamic may not be considered the most salient characterization of the identity of the community that results from this process (unless we are ready to consider that Muslims living as citizens of European societies are less Islamic than those living in Islamic countries). And with this in mind, it is necessary to question the need to consider Islamization as a staggered process, in the way of Eaton and Insoll (see Chapter 2). If Islamization is the creation of Con-Text for both Muslims and non-Muslims, surely it does not have an end or stages? A community can have a more or less extensive Con-Text *in loco*, but it certainly cannot be purer or more complete in its Islamization.⁵

Context and Con-Text

In the next section I will look with some detail at cases of relationships between context and Con-Text. Among the reviewed cases, there are commonly accepted signs used to represent Islam or some aspects of it. The purpose of this section is to explore how the different meanings of the same cultural element can play different roles and in turn can shape Islamic identity.

We can start with the name of Islam itself. The word *islām* has a previous meaning that can be explained with the idea of 'peaceful submission' (see Chapter 1). It is through a process of creation of Con-Text that *islām* (peaceful submission) becomes Islam (the Religion, or *al-Dīn*) in a very particular historical and cultural context, to the point that it is difficult to imagine a different meaning for the word nowadays. The same phenomenon happens to other signs: they can have a long trajectory of being associated with very different meanings before their Islamization. An example of this is the iconographic Crescent and Star, used as a symbol of Islam (although unrecognized by Islamic scholars) originally by their association with the Ottoman dynasty after the conquest of Constantinople. Before that, it had been associated as a signifier to many deities, royal houses and cities in the Middle East and Mediterranean before the arrival of Islam, among them Byzantium, from which it eventually passed to the Ottomans. All those previous meanings, however, have been forgotten nowadays (Ridgeway 1908). But previous meanings do not always disappear; in some cases, they remain, and they even reinforce the Islamic meaning attributed to the sign, without detriment to their previous attributions. An example of this would be the Khamsa symbol, also called Fatima's Hand in Islamic contexts. The sign is a representation of a hand, sometimes with inscriptions or accompanied by the drawing of an eye in the palm. The history of the Khamsa is very long in the Old World, and particularly in the Middle East and North Africa, always related to apotropaic magic and protection against the Evil Eye. The symbol was Islamized by associating it with the Prophet and Fāṭima al-Zahrāʾ, his daughter and wife of ʿAlī, through (not universally accepted) historical narratives. Another way in which the sign was linked to Islam was by establishing a parallel between the five fingers and the Five Pillars of Islam (declaration of faith, prayer, almsgiving, fasting and pilgrimage). Its use continues also in Jewish and Christian traditions, with the same attributes of magical protection, but interestingly the hand in these traditions is related to other female characters: Rachel and the Virgin Mary. Diane Apostolos-Cappadona has reasonably suggested that this feminine association goes back to the pre-Islamic uses of the symbol and it is due to its predominance in contexts associated with female bodily functions (conception, lactation, childbearing, etc). However, the Khamsa can also be found associated with representations of dynastical power, such as the Nasrids of the Kingdom of Granada in al-Andalus (thirteenth to fifteenth centuries CE) (Apostolos-Cappadona 2005; Silva Santa-Cruz 2013).

A more complex, but even more illustrative case of Islamization is the intimate association of the Arabic language with Islam. As the native language of Muḥammad, in which the Quran was first recited and then written, Arabic became a sign of identity for Muslims, who were in turn closely identified with the Arabs in the first stages of Islamic history. The first Arabic inscriptions of the Islamic period include clear indications of the professed identity (and beliefs) of the authors (Hoyland 1997: 687–95; 2006). Arabic was the language of the Arabs, but it was also the language of the Muslims. From 691 CE, the construction of the Dome of the Rock in Jerusalem under the Caliphate of ʿAbd al-Mālik, clearly indicated the position of Islam as the supreme religion, in inscriptions inspired in the Quranic *sūras* and written in Arabic. The *shahāda* (i.e. the declaration of faith: 'There is no god but Allāh and Muḥammad is His Prophet'), written in Arabic also, started to figure prominently in the aniconic Umayyad coins, initiating a style that is still used today.

And finally, other Arabic inscriptions appear to display the relevance of Islam (Hoyland 1997: 695–703; 2006; Johns 2003).

From its Islamization, the Arabic language would become part of the Islamic Con-Text and would become itself a key drive for Islamization, even for non-Muslims. The implication of Arabic as the language not only of Muslims, but as the language of power and high culture, enhanced and reinforced this Islamization. Even if the early Islamic state apparatus of the Umayyads was supported by Greek-speaking civil servants (Robinson 2010: 212–13), there is clear evidence of the active role of Arabs in taking control of the mechanisms of power (Sijpestejn 2007) and developing an elite culture (Hillenbrand 1982).

We can see an example of the Con-Textual Arabic facilitating in turn further expansion of Con-Text in al-Andalus in the ninth century. In this period, there is clear documentation showing that the local bishops were complaining about the fashion between Mozarabs (Christians living among Muslims in Iberia) to adopt cultural traits of the Muslim Arabs: not only did they speak and write in Arabic, but they enjoyed the same literature and taste and dressed in the same way. Although they did not abandon Christianity, Church scholars complained that they were losing their own identity in favour of that of the Muslims (Simonet 1983 [1897], II: 367–71). This did not only happen in Cordoba itself. We know about al-Ablī, a poet in the town of Ilbīra, near Granada, who was famous for his proficiency in Arabic poetry and who used a *nisba* as his daily name, in a pure Arabic fashion (al-Ablī means 'the one from Abla'). Al-Ablī, famous contender in poetry festivals, fought in the *Fitna* wars of al-Andalus in the late-ninth century against the side of the Arab Muslims, and thus he was part of an alliance that included Christians and recently converted Muslims at least. We cannot be sure about al-Ablī's religious affiliation, but we do know that he came originally from a village with a Latin name: Abla is in South East Spain, half way between Granada and Almeria, in an area where Latin toponyms are the norm. So, it is very possible that al-Ablī was a Christian himself, or at least had some Christian ancestry or relationships. In any case, it is clear that his poetry skills in Arabic were celebrated by Christians and

Muslims alike. This was eventually the cause of his downfall, because his Arab enemies remembered all too well his artistic taunts and had him executed in the later years of the conflict (Ibn Ḥayyān 1937: 63–4; 1952: 155–60). Al-Ablī and his poetry represent another case of cultural adoption of Arabic language and Arab taste in the background of the Christian community of the area of Ilbīra. Under a different paradigm, the cases of Cordoba and Ilbīra could be considered as a process of Arabization without conversion to Islam, rather than Islamization. Under Ahmed's theory, it certainly fits the definition of Con-Text. Even if the very same identity of 'Mozarab' represents in itself a rejection of the belief in Islam, the fact that the representation itself is expressed with the adoption of, or even with the resistance to adopt, specific elements of Islamic identity, make it intelligible in its Con-Text, and therefore *Islamic*.

One more telling case can be made with respect to mosques. These are to a large extent the epitomes of Islam, as they are a key marker of Muslim identity, and at the same time provide a context for many other markers. Among many other things, mosques are ideal places for praying and offer a clear indication of the *qibla*, the direction towards Mecca. They are usually decorated with inscriptions, with the *shahāda* (declaration of faith) in a predominant position, and contain libraries with copies of the Quran and other works of the rich Islamic tradition. One can also find in them calendars, tables and clocks that are used to establish with precision the times to pray and the different rituals spread over the year. It is often from minarets in the mosques where the call for prayer is done. Their central role, however, is to provide a point of contact for all community members among themselves and with their local imam, their guide. In a proper context, mosques are a symbol not only of Muslim identity, but of the whole context of identity in itself. There, Muslims learn to be Muslims by participating in rituals and activities and by listening to doctrinal explanations. It is no wonder that mosques are considered the best archaeological markers for the presence of a Muslim community, as they acquired their essential elements very early in Islamic history (Johns 1999), and have changed very little, despite the development of regional and local traditions in different periods. In archaeological contexts, mosques have even been used for measuring the size of their respective communities (Walmsley and Damgaard 2005).

However, like any other sign, the meaning of mosques really depends on their context and Con-Text, as they can become invested with very different meanings. I am not only referring to cases where buildings initially conceived as mosques cease to be mosques because they are consciously repurposed as something else (such as the case of the Mosque of Cordoba in Spain, now a Christian cathedral, or Hagia Sophia in Istanbul, first a church, then a mosque and temporarily turned into a museum before becoming a mosque again). There are cases where active mosques are not necessarily seen as a symbol of the identity of Muslims living in their vicinity, and therefore can be considered outside of the Con-Text *in loco* of that particular place. An example can be set with a particular experience that I had in Southern Albania in the summer of 2010. I was leading a small survey project for the remains of the post-medieval period in the National Park of Butrint. Around the archaeological site of Butrint and at the southern side of the Vivari Channel there are three villages surrounding the plain of Vrina representing different religious communities: Catholic and Orthodox Christians and Muslims. One of the three villages, Xarrë, was interesting for me for two reasons. In the first place, it was the oldest village according to historical maps and documents from as early as the eighteenth century, in which it appeared as the first Ottoman position beyond the limits of Butrint, a Venetian possession at that time.[6] Secondly, it featured a small but prominent mosque in the highest point of the village, clearly visible from all the places around it. All this suggested that there was an important Muslim community in Xarrë, perhaps surviving since the Ottoman period, although it was also possible that the Muslim community was a product of the Çam immigration in the early-twentieth century.[7]

We visited Xarrë with the intention of finding archaeological evidence and local informants that could help to clarify these questions.[8]

We chose a Friday to visit the mosque, expecting to find people who would be interested in sharing stories about these issues. To our surprise, the mosque had no attendants at the praying time beyond a lonely imam who came late and kindly allowed us to visit the building and the surroundings while he prayed alone and hurriedly. He did not call for pray (*adhān*), despite having a minaret that was possibly equipped with loudspeakers. In my visits to other Islamic countries, mosques would be well-attended on a Friday at the main praying time; in places with large communities, people would have to line up outside the mosque to perform their prayers. The Muslim communities of the Balkans are less sizeable than those of the Middle East, but Friday prayers are still usually well-attended events. It was not possible to know how large the Muslim community of Xarrë was, but local informants indicated that many people in the village are Muslims. The lack of *adhān* was also surprising. Although the call for prayer may be restricted by law in some places, I had observed that in Gjirokastër, a nearby Albanian town, the call from minarets was loud and clear, and in Arabic.

A member of our team was from Greece, and he was able to engage in very friendly talks with the local population, which was Greek- and Albanian-speaking.[9] Conversations with Orthodox locals gave us interesting information that was later on confirmed by the imam of the mosque to a large extent. All the inhabitants of Xarrë claimed to be descendants of families living there since the Middle Ages, originally from a nearby village, now disappeared. This place was called Zaropoula in eighteenth-century maps and Palaeospitia (Greek for 'Old Houses') by them. Our survey of this site and later archaeological work by Ilir Parangoni (2015) has shown that the village seems to have been abandoned during the late Ottoman period (eighteenth to nineteenth centuries CE in Albania). From that period there is a coexistence (and even intermarriages) between Muslims and Orthodox families in the village, although more Muslims arrived with the Çam immigrations.

The link between the Muslim community and the mosque was very interesting. The local Muslims did not attend the mosque, allegedly because of doctrinal differences and because it was funded by a foreign fund (probably Turkish or Saudi, but that was not confirmed) that had imposed the imam, a Çam born in Philiates (Greece). The mosque was Sunnī, while the predominant form of Islam in Southern Albania is Bektashism, an order of Shīʿa Alevism with relevant doctrinal and ritual differences (Doja 2004). The foundation of the mosque had occurred approximately ten years before our visit, and the Muslim population of Xarrë had clearly not adopted it as a symbolic place for them. There does not seem to be an earlier mosque than that, though. We were told that the Çams that arrived in the village had set up mosques in huts in the lower parts of the village, but nothing remained of them. The Muslims of the village, therefore, did not have a proper mosque, and some of them prayed in the local church of St Nicholas. This is not inconsistent with the practices of Bektashis, who tend to reject canonical rituals of Islam and support instead a personal spiritual connection with God (Doja 2004: 464–9). This close relationship between the two communities could also have been a response to the aggressive attitude to religion of the Communist dictatorship of Enver Hoxha (1946–1991). In 1967, the state started an offensive against the material bases of religion that involved the destruction of numerous churches and mosques and culminated in the 1976 Constitution that declared Albania an atheist state (Mustafa 2008: 59–64).

The example of the link between the mosque and the Muslim community of Xarrë shows clearly why it is important to understand the relationships between context, Con-Text *in toto* and Con-Text *in loco*. In this particular case, the mosque *as the space of prayer of the community* was not part of the Con-Text *in loco* of the Muslims of Xarrë but was part of the Con-Text *in toto* of the region. A less informed approach could have concluded that the lack of mosque users meant that there were no Muslims in Xarrë, but that would have been false. The truth is that the Muslims of Xarrë, with the possible exception of the Çam imam of the mosque, had meaningfully agreed on their disagreement with the version of Islam that the new mosque of the village represented, and therefore rejected it as their own space for prayer. What remains to help us understand the Con-Text of this village is to locate the symbols of Muslim identity. My research was too superficial to achieve that, but good starting points for this question would be the specific slots for Muslims in the cemetery of the village (noted by a local informant), the family lineages and the history of St Nicholas Church, besides possible symbols kept in private contexts.

Being Islamic and the archaeology of Islamization

In this chapter I have started from the implication of the assertion that Islam cannot be defined only as a core of doctrinal beliefs and practices or as a cultural system without belief, but as a medium to allow mutual intelligibility between Islamic identities. From there I have gone on to explore the concept of Islamic identities from the evolutionary point of view defined by Gabrielle Marranci, based on feelings. The core idea of this perspective is that all identities are essentially formed in the mind of individuals who, despite their biological condition of individuality, are connected between themselves and the material world by the processes of their neurological system. As much as Marranci's work has to commend, his perspective is limited by a certain idealism because of his mind-matter dualism and by an ultimate lack of connection with Islamic belief specifically. In my opinion, these problems can be overcome by using the less individualistic, but clearly Islamic-focused theory of Shahab Ahmed.

Ahmed's theory in *Being Islamic* defines Islam as a field defined by Text, Pre-Text and Con-Text and an enabling of meaningful and intelligible identification and, especially, disagreement between Islamic people. It presents a clear challenge for the archaeological research of Islamization because it implies ultimately that there are no unequivocal signs of Islam, valid for all Con-Texts *in loco*. The work of the archaeologist researching Islamization, therefore, consists not of finding (new) markers of Islam, but on explaining historically how those markers came to be (that is, how Con-Text was created).

This is not unexpected from an archaeological point of view. After all, archaeological theory has tackled the question of identities from different points of view in the last forty years. This has allowed archaeologists to move from essentially normative approaches, based on the association between identities and particular traits of material culture (Trigger 2006: 211–313), to more sophisticated perspectives that consider identities as parts of a social system related to material culture in ways that are not unilineal and straightforward (cf. Conlin Casella and Fowler 2005; Insoll 2007; Jones 1997; Meskell 2002). What is required, therefore, is to understand the ways in which material culture and Islamic Con-Text relate, and the ways in which archaeologists can endeavour to establish these connections. This requires us to consider different archaeological approaches to material culture, and this is what I will do in the next chapter.

4

Islamic Things, Islamic Beings and Con-Text

Introduction: Islamic meaning in the world

In the previous chapter I moved the focus of Islamization from the transformation of identities (i.e. from non-Islamic to Islamic identities) to the becoming of Islamic human beings in consonance with the work of Shahab Ahmed. The Islamic human being is defined by the search for knowledge about the Revelation, a task that is accomplished with the production of Islamic meaning about the Text (the Islamic Meaning and Truth as presented in the sacred texts) and Pre-Text (the Islamic Meaning and Truth as deduced in the organization of the cosmos). This production of meaning departs from and produces Islamic Con-Text, so that it is possible to say, with Ahmed, that Con-Text or Islam precedes Muslims. In this chapter I am going to take a step forward from that thought and suggest that, in fact, Islam not only precedes, but also *produces* Muslims (and, by extension, Islamic beings, Muslims or not). This is a tenet that Ahmed would not necessarily uphold and I am going to justify carefully with current archaeological theory.

The idea that Islam produces believers should not be confused with the fallacy that Muslims can only act within the confines of the behaviour defined by (any) Islamic orthodoxy. As I have explained in the previous chapters, Islam in its widest sense encompasses a vast field between faith, meaning and action that escapes the confines of orthodoxy and allows space for variety, disagreement and contradiction in an intelligible fashion. In Ahmed's theory, the defining feature of a Muslim is to search for God's Revelation to Muḥammad in the world, thus giving it meaning and bringing it into Con-Text. But at the same time, a Muslim is the result of the previous Con-Text, since it is there where Muslims find the means to reach their interpretation. It follows that Con-Text (or Islam, to simplify) has to be somehow part of the world where (or *in* which) Con-Textual meaning can be inscribed, stored, transmitted, absorbed and reinterpreted. The question that I try to answer in this chapter is how that can happen. In other words, how is Islam manifested in the world?

Insoll has defined Islam as a superstructure composed of structuring principles (1999: 1). He believes that religion (not only Islam) is manifested in all aspects of existence (2004), so a question about how this influence works can be raised. In more recent works, Insoll has showed interest in Ian Hodder's entanglement theory (Hodder 2012, in Insoll 2015: 6; 2020: 433) to explain how the particular qualities of materials can help to transmit particular meaning, although he has not defined any particular example for Islamization. Hodder's entanglements are part of a set of recent developments of archaeological theory on materiality that have emerged following Latour's work.

Although not related to Islam, the work of Timothy Pauketat *Archaeology of Cosmos* (2012), is another interesting approach to the question of the links between materiality and religious meaning. Pauketat introduces the concept of *bundle* as a set of materials with specific meanings that together acquire and transmit a very different meaning. The term he uses is inspired by the bundles of Native American shamans that allowed them a special communication with spirits. Pauketat expands the concept and defines bundles as specific configurations of elements of the world, including celestial phenomena, orientations, landscapes, architectural features, practices, etc. from which religious meaning *emerges* as a result of the specific meshworks of all these different elements. Besides his evident inspiration on Native American ideas, Pauketat's approach to materiality is post-Latourian in scope.

In the following pages I am going to present very succinctly some aspects of the current archaeological debate on materiality that I consider relevant to my quest of Islamization in this book. I will then discuss Islamic Truth and Meaning from the perspective of one of these new approaches, new materialism.

Things as emerging from relationships and new materialism

In the most recent decades, the traditional conventions of the archaeological debate have been deeply transformed by the introduction in the discipline of anthropological perspectives derived from the sociological critique to modernity started by Bruno Latour (1993) [1991]. In archaeology, this influence was combined with changes in other disciplines, such as the ontological turn in anthropological studies or postcolonial studies in literary theory (see Crellin 2020; Harris 2021; Harris and Cipolla 2017; Jervis 2018 for a useful introduction to the impact of these changes in archaeological theories).

At the centre of this debate there is the concept of relationality: things are not defined from their own essential qualities, but from the perspective of the relationships that they establish with other things. The focus on relationality began with Latour's question of Cartesian dualism between subjects (people) and objects. Latour showed that people and things are an outcome of the cultural relationships established between them. There is no difference between nature and culture, but a continuous interaction between people and things that actively produces new people and new things. History does not depend on the agency of people over objects, but rather on the development of new relationships between 'actants' (people or things). This is called 'Actor-Network Theory' and in archaeology it has given rise to 'symmetrical archaeology', which advocates the placement of things at the centre of archaeological enquiry (Olsen 2007; 2010; Olsen et al 2012; Shanks 2007; Webmore 2007; Witmore 2007). The networks of Actor-Network Theory and symmetrical archaeology are a good example of the focus on relationality, as are the meshworks suggested by Tim Ingold (2007; 2011) and the entanglement theory of Ian Hodder (2012; 2016). The latter is particularly interesting, as it allows us to define history as the universe of relationships established by different actants, growing with increasing networks of entanglements with new people and things in time and space. This makes this theory compatible with Ahmed's Con-Text. As noted above, Insoll has echoed entanglement theory in his latest approaches to Islamization. However, that is not the perspective that I espouse here, because I believe that it does not consider a very important concept to its full extent: I am talking about flat ontology.

Flat ontology is the next step beyond relationality. It is an ontological approach where assumed dualisms in social sciences (culture/nature, human/thing, mind/body) are flattened. What is questioned is not the existence of these dualisms, but rather their consideration as given, as essential, and their centrality to the set of relationships that give rise to materiality and sociality. 'New materialism' is the theoretical perspective that stems from the concept of flat ontology. New materialists are interested in how objects become precisely defined by the assemblage of the relationships between the inherent qualities of the substances of which they are made, and the people and things that interact with them at specific moments. In many senses this approach was inaugurated in archaeology with a paper written by Tim Ingold, where the anthropologist showed the importance of the vibrancy of the substances of which materials are made (2007). Archaeologists started looking at the ways in which assemblages are in a continuous process of becoming something different by their engagement with new people, things or assemblages They found inspiration on the flat ontology of the works of scholars such as Manuel DeLanda (2016) and Jane Bennet (2010), and ultimately on the philosophy of Giles Deleuze and Felix Guattari (Deleuze 1990; [1969]; 1994 [1968]; Deleuze and Guattari 1983 [1977]; 1987 [1980]). Archaeological approaches based on new materialism are recent and include Conneller 2011; 2017; Crellin 2017; 2020; Fowler 2013; 2017; Hamilakis 2017; Harris 2014; 2017; 2021; Jervis 2017a; 2017b; 2018; Jones 2017; Lucas 2012; 2017; Meirion Jones 2017, amongst others (for a wider review, see Harris and Cipolla 2017: 138–46).[1]

As I will explain in the pages that follow, I have found that the perspective of flat ontology from Deleuzean philosophy offers many relevant insights for my purpose in this book. In the following section I will take an approach mainly based on three Deleuzean texts: *Difference and Repetition* (1994 [1968] and the two volumes of *Capitalism and Schizophrenia*: *Anti-Oedipus* (Deleuze and Guattari 1983 [1977]) and *A Thousand Plateaus* (Deleuze and Guattari 1987 [1980]). My reading is enriched by the interpretations of Rachel Crellin (2020), Oliver Harris (2021) and Ben Jervis (2018), and is influenced by the views of other new materialist archaeologists, such as Chris Fowler (2017) and Andrew Meirion Jones (2017). To clarify, I am going to adopt Deleuze's metaphysics to address the concept of ontology in its philosophical sense. In doing so, I will explore how that helps to address my questions about Islamization.

Defining Islamic things

The key question that I am addressing in this section is to understand how things can become part of Con-Text in Ahmed's terms, which is the same as asking how things can be Islamic. What do we mean by an 'Islamic thing'? How can we use this to further our knowledge of Islamization? Or to put it in another way, what is Islamization from the point of view of things?

Let us start from what is probably the simplest and most intuitive conception of ontology nowadays, which is based on identity and representation (Deleuze 1994 [1968]: 1–27). In order to dip straight into the question, let us examine two Islamic objects in particular: a mosque and an Islamic bowl. I have selected the Al-Aqṣā Mosque in the Haram al-Sharīf (the Noble Sanctuary, on the Temple Mount) of Jerusalem (Figure 4.1), and the vessel with an inventory number 21/1965 of the David Collection (Copenhagen), a white opaque, tin-glazed bowl with a blue painted inscription ('made by Abū-l-Baqī' is the Museum's reading), made in Iraq (probably Basra), in the ninth century CE (Figure 4.2).[2]

Figure 4.1 Al-Aqṣā Mosque between 1940 and 1946 (Matson Collection, Library of Congress of the USA, Public Domain).

Figure 4.2 Bowl 21/1965 of the David Collection. Image by Pernille Klemp. Courtesy of the David Collection, Copenhagen.

Are these objects Islamic? The answer is obviously yes, as the quality of being Islamic was one of the requested conditions to choose them. But that condition is implicit in the idea of the Al-Aqṣā Mosque, whereas I needed to make it explicit when invoking object 21/1965 of the David Collection. In fact, if we compare the generic concepts *mosque* and *bowl*, this difference appears most evident: the *mosque* is by definition a sacred space for Muslims, and it is therefore intimately linked to Islamic Meaning and Truth (in Ahmed's words). The bowl, however, has no intrinsic connection to Islam, and cannot be considered to be Islamic unless mediated by a contingent set of relationships.[3] The initial problem that emerges for an archaeologist here is evident: how can we identify an Islamic object if its Islamic quality (its link to Islamic Meaning and Truth) is not contained in the definition of the object itself? Will we always be able to identify the contingent relationships that make it Islamic?

The problem does not end there, it becomes more complicated. Let us think of the Mosque of Cordoba (Spain). The building was originally a congregational mosque in 786 under the patronage of the Emir ʿAbd al-Raḥmān I al-Dākhil, and subsequently expanded under other rulers until the tenth century CE. After the conquest of Cordoba by the Christian Crown of Castile, the mosque became a cathedral in 1238, and it has kept this denomination since. Technically, the Mosque of Cordoba cannot now be considered a mosque, because it is not used for Muslim worship. However, its denomination as a mosque is still kept in part because of tradition and in part as a political claim.[4] The strength of tradition and politics is even clearer in the case of the Mosque of Hagia Sofia in Istanbul (Turkey). It was not always a mosque: in the place where the building is today there used to be the Church of the Holy Wisdom of God, first dedicated in 360 CE. The current building was erected by order of the Byzantine Emperor Justinian in 532–537 CE and was, during almost one thousand years, the largest Christian Cathedral in the world, the epitome of Byzantine architecture. It did not become a mosque until the conquest of Constantinople by the Ottomans in 1453. It ceased to be a mosque in 1931 under Atatürk's secularist policies, and became a museum in 1935. It reverted to being a mosque in 2020, in a political move designed by the Islamist government of Recep Tayyip Erdoğan (Guerin 2020). The case of Hagia Sophia shows how the idea of the mosque was kept alive as a memory for almost a century, until it was actualized again. The concept of *mosque* is used in the cases of Cordoba and Istanbul with a similar but different value than the discussion above. In this case, it is the quality of Islamic itself that needs to be modified by contingent relationships. This seems counterintuitive, as intrinsic qualities should in principle be present or not present.

To summarize, two problems seem to emerge from this short discussion in relation to Islamic archaeology. On the one hand, concepts such as *bowl* are too wide to capture the reality of Islamic things and leave archaeologists with the need to specify. On the other hand, concepts such as *mosque* are too specific and require an expansion of the quality of Islamic that accompanies the concept in some particular circumstances. Certainly, languages have modifiers to deal with these circumstances, but that is nothing short of a recognition that this is a more general problem with the whole idea of concepts attached to things of which our Islamic mosque and bowl are simply a particular example.

For Deleuze, this problem is a manifestation of the ontology of identity and representation that has dominated Western thought since the times of Aristotle. Deleuze believes that there are multiple issues in an ontology based on the existence of discrete beings (or *things*) defined by their *haecceity*, *quiddity* or *thisness*, that is, the result of the set of properties that make a thing exactly consistent with what it is. He dedicates a complete work, *Difference and Repetition*, to the deconstruction of this ontology and proposes at the same time the basis of a different ontology not based on identity and representation, but on – precisely – difference and repetition (1994 [1968]). In *Capitalism and Schizophrenia* (1983 [1977] and 1987[1980]), Deleuze and Guattari combine insights from multiple philosophical, psychological, historical, scientific and literary insights that go beyond ontology and try to present a perspective to understand existence from different points of view. Deleuze considers that the reality is dependent on a single entity (hence a flat ontology) that manifests itself in different modes and with different intensities. The perception of these modes and intensities depends on three different syntheses of the processes of repetition with passive and active versions. These syntheses are the habit, the memory and what we would call the promise of the eternal return. They are also responsible for the generation of the perception of individuality (particularly in their passive versions) and time (1994 [1968]; see also an admirable discussion adjusted to archaeology in Harris 2021: 208–14).

The metaphysical conception of Deleuze makes the study of the world challenging, as the concepts based on identity and representation cannot be used. Deleuze and Guattari propose instead a new way of approaching it: the assemblage. The concept of assemblage is intuitively easy to understand. To put it in the way in which DeLanda describes it, we can give an escalated definition (2016: 9–21). The first thing that we need to understand is that an assemblage is a historically unique set of interrelated elements with emergent qualities that come into play as a result of the internal relationships of all the elements of the set. There is no essential element within the assemblage; all of them contribute to the totality on the same grounds. Haecceity in this perspective is not a result of intrinsic qualities of the assemblage (it has none) but emerges out of the property of the assemblage to be a unique event. In this way Deleuze rescues a fundamental metaphysical concept but frees it from its links to transcendent identity.

A thought experiment can be proposed with Bowl 21/1965 of the David Collection. Let us think of that bowl as an assemblage of elements. Those elements are a flaring rim, a body with a roughly semi-globular profile, a flat base, an inscription, a white tin-based glazed cover ... None of them defines the totality, but together they all create the object that has the qualities that allow us to define it as a finely decorated bowl from the Islamic period. Two observations that pertain to the concept of assemblage follow from this experiment. The first one is that the assemblage is equivalent to an object in itself (it has qualities). The second one is that the components of the assemblage have an identity in themselves, but the assemblage is something that goes beyond the addition of its parts: it is a different, new object whose qualities emerge out of the totality.

Let us extend our thought experiment by imagining that we can physically break Bowl 21/1965 and look at the fragments. Every fragment is now a ceramic sherd, all of them with glazed surfaces, but they also show their internal fabric in the breaks. Some sherds are fragments of what they used to be the rim, others are walls and there are others that were part of the base. They all form an assemblage that is slightly different to the bowl, because it is now a broken bowl. And still, the assemblage is a single object, a set of ceramic sherds that show the emergent quality of being a potential bowl (in the past, before it was broken up, and in the future, if the sherds are stuck together again). The sherds themselves are single objects, but in this example it is easier to see another important characteristic of the assemblages: their components are not only objects in themselves, but they can also become members of other assemblages. So, the rim sherds can be taken as part of a series of rims of similar vessels to become part of a typology, the sherds with decoration can be isolated to become part of a catalogue and any of the sherds can be used for a number of destructive analyses to understand the composition and texture of the fabric of the bowl. This case shows that one assemblage is composed of many different assemblages, shares elements with other assemblages and can be part of others at the same time. Bowl 21/1965 or its fragments would still be part of the David Collection, an assemblage located in a building in Copenhagen. The bowl or its fragments are also members of the Opaque White Glaze type, as defined in Kennet 2004, an assemblage composed of all the vessels produced with the same processes and techniques as our example (cf. Fowler 2017; Jervis 2018: 83–91).

Deleuze would insist that all these assemblages coexist in the same plane of existence as everything that we consider real, including the Al-Aqṣā Mosque, Bowl 21/1965 and the book (or computer) that the reader is using to look at these lines. There are no aggregates and basic elements, there are only relationships of interiority (those that define the assemblage as an event) and relationships of exteriority (defined by the emergent qualities of the assemblage); it is important to remember that the concepts of interiority and exteriority are relative, dependent on the separate consideration of each assemblage. This flat ontology cannot be represented with the concepts that we shape in our mind, because they are based on an ontology of identity and representation. In order to understand assemblages with instruments that are not concepts, Deleuze and Guattari propose two metaphors: the map (Deleuze and Guattari 1987 [1980]: 12–13; 39–74;[5] cf. 2018: 67) and the pair virtual-actual or problem-solution (Deleuze 1994 [1968]: 168–221; Hughes 2009: 111–14; cf. De Landa 2016: 165–88; Harris 2021: 52–5; Jervis 2018: 57–8).[6]

An assemblage can be mapped rather than conceptualized because it is always composed of populations of specific individuals. The assemblage of all the mosques in history is not the same as the concept of a *mosque*, as the former is composed of specific mosques, whereas the latter is an abstract or generic concept applied to particular buildings. Archaeologists are familiar with the idea of mapping, drawing, sketching and planning phases of excavation or building façades as the best way to convey the information they contain. The same method can be metaphorically applied to assemblages, even when they seem to be composed of incommensurable quantities of specific elements. Like the map, an assemblage is not the territory, but it does indicate the relationships established between its different elements. Deleuze offers several ideas to map assemblages, of which the most relevant are territorialization and coding. The territorialization of the map indicates the areas in which the assemblage has more intensity, more actuality (territorialized areas) and those in which the assemblage loses intensity (deterritorializes) and is more prone to establish relationships with other assemblages to form new assemblages (areas of reterritorialization). Territorializing and deterritorializing areas are connected by lines of flight that indicate the change vectors of intensity. For example, for a believer, the Mosque of al-Aqṣā would have the point of highest territorialization in its *miḥrāb*, the small apse on the southern wall that indicates the *qibla*, the direction of Mecca to which prayer must be directed. Areas of deterritorialization of the mosque, however, would be the walls and the gates, where the space of the building finds its limits.

Codes are different to areas of territorialization, because they are not about intensity but about meaning. They are the forms of expression of organization in the assemblage and can be represented as the marks of the map that allow us to understand how the territory is structured. For example, contour lines in a standard territorial map are the code used to indicate height (which is the 'intensity' in this example); in contrast, the lines of flight in the maps would be the gradient lines connecting the tops of mountains with the bottoms of valleys, which would be areas of different territoriality. To understand how codes work in the Al-Aqṣā Mosque, we need to consider its layout, with seven bays roughly orientated to the south, where the *miḥrāb* of the building is. These are the codes used to point the believer in the direction of prayer.

It is important to emphasize that the relationships between areas of territorialization and codes are always relative: codes can act as ways of territorializing and ways of territorializing may be transformed in codes. Archaeologists may look at the Al-Aqsa Mosque in a very different way from believers because they establish very different types of relationships. The different coding elements of the mosque – bays, columns, *miḥrāb* – can be classified in typologies, therefore making them part of different assemblages. The different fabrics of the building become coding elements that guide the phasing of the mosque in separate periods, and thus archaeologists can engage with yet another range of assemblages (one for each phase at least).

An example with different mosques can be given. Jeffrey Fleisher (2019)[7] has demonstrated that the materials used in the construction of the mosques in Swahili stone-cities along their history are charged with meaning with regard to the relationship of local Islam to other traditional beliefs and the landscapes associated to those. The materials used for the construction of mosques changed in time as the practices of Islam became more standardized and related to the urban landscape of the stone-cities. Fleisher explains how these mosques can be considered part of wider assemblages and territorialize along the lines of flight created by their building materials. So, on the one hand, we can consider the Swahili mosques as assemblages in themselves, and look at the different fabrics of buildings as coded in particular ways. On the other hand, we can consider the mosques within the Islamic Con-Textual assemblage *in loco* and consider the fabrics within the lines of flight, places where particular syncretic beliefs territorialize.

The other metaphor that we can take from Deleuze's writings to define an assemblage is that it is the solution to a problem. In the ontology of Deleuze, a problem is an Idea, an empty structure that exists as a virtual object that guides the creation of the actual object. Virtual objects emerge in the assemblages by a process that Deleuze calls *differen*tiation, whereas actual events emerge from a process that he defines as *differen*ciation (cf. Harris 2021: 54–5). For Deleuze, the virtual and the actual are two states of reality. The former represents a problem, that is, an empty structure, and the other the solution, that is, the content of that structure. The main difference between problem and solution, or between differen*t*iation and differen*c*iation, as Deleuze indicates, it is that of the intensity of the being in the object. The concept of intensity can be used to characterize the forces that produce differenciation in the being.[8] An object reaches its maximum intensity of being when it becomes completely actual (differen*c*iated). Conversely, when the object is not entirely actual, it is susceptible to growth in intensity around the potentialities of its structure. In other words, when an object is not completely actual, there is a discrepancy between the structure that the object is called to fill in and the content that is available, and therefore the rest of the structure is only virtual, pure potential. If we revisit our broken Bowl 21/1965, we can continue our thought experiment and perform a very simple exercise that every archaeologist has done at least once. The reader must select two random sherds of the fragmented bowl and forget the rest. It is very important to comment that in this thought experiment the bowl in its entirety is not there, but there are only two sherds of a ceramic vessel. Now the reader must look at the two sherds and try to think of the vessel of which they were part. The vessel searched for is a problem, an empty structure, and the sherds constitute an assemblage that is the solution to the problem. As archaeologists do, the reader can use the sherds to reconstruct the form of the vessel in their mind, to draw it, and to record any other characteristics that would have been part of it. Looking carefully at the assemblage, however, the reader will note that there are ways in which the reconstructed vessel could diverge from the original bowl. If the fragments do not allow the reader to have a full profile of the vessel (that is, a full line from the rim to the base), then they will not be able to know its height and will have to estimate it. If the sherds do not include the full inscription at the centre of the bowl, then the reader will need to complete it with their imagination, and they could misspell the words. Finally, if the selected fragments belong only to the wall of the vessel and do not contain any other relevant features, then the reader might not even be able to tell if the original object was a bowl! What we can see here is that an assemblage of two sherds is offering (differentiating) a multiplicity of solutions to the problem of the vessel. The main difference between the assemblage of two sherds and the complete bowl before it was broken is that the latter is an actual (differenciated) object, and the former is an object that has some actuality (the sherds) and the potential to become the vessel-structure in many differentiated ways.

One way to understand how the virtual can be differentiated in assemblages is to look at the process of folding and stratification of different assemblages. We have seen above that assemblages are connected by lines of flight and areas of territorialization and deterritorialization. But assemblages can also have vertical relationships of depth. Deleuze and Guattari introduce strata in the second chapter of *A Thousand Plateaus* (1987 [1980]: 39–74). For DeLanda, a stratum is a strongly territorialized assemblage (2016: 23), and Jervis considers them the elements that assemblages connect and at the same time the bases from which assemblages deterritorialize and reterritorialize (Jervis 2018: 62–5). Deleuze and Guattari warn indeed that assemblages and strata are the same, and that their only difference lies in their roles, which can be exchanged. Following Harris, we can say that assemblages and strata are folded together (Harris 2014). Any assemblage is the interface between two strata: one of them is the stratum that acts as a diferentiation system for Ideas; the other one is the stratum that comes from the plane of consistency (Deleuze and Guattari 1987 [1980]: 40), which is a name frequently used by Deleuze and Guattari to refer to the plane where the intensity of being originates. In this figure, an assemblage is formed by the pressure of a stratum, the intensity of being, over another stratum that gives a shape to the virtual. The stratum itself is a second assemblage, but it is used as a cast in the field of the virtual to create the Idea-structure where the first assemblage acquires actuality and potential.

The main interest of the concept of the stratum is that it gives us a way to go beyond the composition of the assemblage to explore its potentialities. For example, besides contemplating the Al-Aqṣā Mosque and Bowl 21/1965 as actual assemblages, we could try to understand how they can fit into wider assemblages. How did the Mosque of Al-Aqṣā relate to the people of Jerusalem in the early Islamic period? How did the Islamic and pre-Crusader structural elements of the mosque conserved today fit with the mosque that was in those periods? How was Bowl 21/1965 made, and how was it used? How did it end up in a museum in Copenhagen? These questions constitute problems, and their solutions lay in the potentialities that they can unleash in the assemblages under consideration, that is, the Al-Aqṣā Mosque and Bowl 21/1965. The strata, in these cases, are the wider, underlying assemblages over which the mosque and bowl can fit and fulfil their potential. In other words, the strata can be modelled as existing structures that shape the 'territory' of the assemblages (differentiation), and with it the course of the lines of flight along which the pass from the virtual to the actual (differenciation) happens.

From the point of view of the above discussion, we can return to the question with which the chapter started: how can we define a thing as Islamic? We can start to answer it by returning to the concept of Islamic Con-Text and redefining it, from the point of view of Deleuzean metaphysics, as an assemblage with a virtual part differentiated as possible manifestations of the Revelation. From this perspective, an

Islamic object is a differenciated, actualized part of the Islamic Con-Textual assemblage. How this differenciation or actualization happens can be ascertained by letting ourselves be guided by the coding structures that express the lines of flight that connect areas of lower and higher territorialization. Coming back to one of our examples above, the bowl of the David Collection is part of the Islamic Con-Text assemblage; it became an Islamic bowl because it was produced and consumed in a context where art and craft were intelligibly perceived as Islamic.

The case of the mosques requires more careful consideration. The Al-Aqṣā Mosque in Jerusalem can be considered an area of high territorialization of the Islamic Con-Text assemblage. However, this mosque was, for a period of time, under Crusader control (1099–1187) and was first a royal palace and horse stable and then the headquarters of the Temple knights. Was it Islamic then? From the perspective of the Islamic Con-Textual assemblage, the question would not be if the mosque was Islamic or not, but how intense its way of being Islamic was. Under non-Muslim control, the mosque was still a building of high significance, but it did not belong to the Muslims during that period. Its intensity as part of the Con-Text was diminished, it had been deterritorialized. The same could be said of the examples of Hagia Sophia between 1931 and 2020 and of the Mosque of Cordoba, mentioned above. This is also the case for Bektashi Muslims when considering the mosque in Xarrë (Albania), mentioned in Chapter 3.

Let us stay in the mosque of Al-Aqṣā of the Crusader period, however. It is a less intensely Islamic mosque, but it must be stressed that the Islamic Con-Textual meaning of the mosque, that which makes it part of the Islamic Con-Text assemblage, does not exhaust its possible meanings. For a Templar knight, the mosque in this period has no Islamic meaning, because he is not intelligibly involved in the Islamic Con-Text; the meaning that he can assign to the mosque would be related to a different assemblage. Paraphrasing Ahmed: the mosque is one, but its potential meanings are more than one. This is because we cannot understand meaning outside of the assemblages, and in this case, this requires us to consider Islamic people within the Con-Text. In other words, the Islamic Con-Text assemblage also encompasses the Islamic people (Muslims or not) that produce it and are produced by it. This co-determination of Con-Text and Islamic beings has been noted in the previous chapter, but it is worth dwelling on it from the theoretical perspective of flat ontology.

Islamic things, Islamic beings

The introduction of flat ontology in the theoretical perspectives of archaeology means more than questioning the central role of the human being in the universe: it means questioning how a human being is constituted. Cartesian dualism, the perspective on which modernity is based, assumes that humanity is an ontological category separated from the rest of the world. Humans, different to other living and non-living entities, are individual beings who aggregate to build communities. This monolithic consideration of humanity as a superior ontological category has been criticized from different perspectives, including biologists, philosophers and other scholars calling for the consideration of humans as part of the living sphere (as part of ecosystems or as determined by the rules of genetics) and anthropologists, psychologists and others searching for ways to blur the line between nature and culture. The ontological turn in anthropology (Harris and Cipolla 2017: 180–5; Cipolla 2020; Jervis 2018: 4–7) paved the way for more radical approaches, and the introduction of Deleuzean philosophy. In Deleuzean metaphysics, human beings emerge from assemblages rather than being determined by their biological condition. This is not to say that there is a denial of the biological aspects of the human being, but they are considered in the combination and stratification of assemblages rather than from a genetic and thus determinant point of view. In other words, *biology alone does not make humans.*

In the previous chapter, I explained how Ahmed establishes a certain historicity of the human condition, since he makes Con-Text precede

Muslims (and by extension, Islamic beings). The departing point of the present chapter was precisely to determine how that is possible, and we have seen how things become Islamic in the assemblages in a way that their meaning can be stored, read and interpreted by Islamic beings. However, the question as set is limited in its scope, since it precludes the range of possible answers to those where meaning, mind, symbol and world are separated categories that intersect in very particular ways (mind reads meaning, meaning is inscribed on symbol, etc.). It is important to remember that this is not a question about symbols in the sense in which Marranci or Geertz, for example, use the concept. From a Deleuzean perspective, the fact that Con-Text precedes the Islamic being cannot be reduced to an act of a person becoming Islamic *after* reading meaning in the Con-Text. Rather, it means that the Islamic being *emerges* out of an assemblage where there are a number of elements that work together to generate that particular result.

In other words, in Deleuzean ontology, there are no differences between the origin of Islamic (human) beings and Islamic things. They all emerge out of the Islamic Con-Text assemblage. It could be argued that, from the perspective of Ahmed, only Islamic humans[9] can generate Con-Text since only they have the previous knowledge to search hermeneutically for Con-Textual meaning. Certainly, it is important to make the point clear that I am taking Ahmed's views where he never attempted to take them and that it would be fair to disagree with me from a different theoretical perspective. However, from a Deleuzean perspective, the answer to this objection is that, if Muslims need to have Con-Textual knowledge to generate Con-Textual meaning, then it is correct to say that Con-Text is integral to the ontological concept of Islamic being (in the same way that one cannot have Con-Text without Islamic beings). In Deleuzean terms, things become through assemblages, and so Islamic beings become (differenciated, actualized), at least in part, by their participation in the Islamic Con-Textual assemblage.

To be clear, the most immediate result of Deleuzean metaphysics is the deconstruction of individual beings in favour of a more distributed conception of Being. This allows us to consider Islamic beings as emerging from their relationships in context, whether they are human or not. It also provides a new perspective on the question of non-Muslims engaging with Con-Text, even if not in search of meaning for themselves: the architect, the potter and the scholar. As I explained above, Ahmed distinguished here the producer (non-Islamic) from the product (Islamic). From a Deleuzean perspective, both the producer and the product emerge as Islamic beings as long as they are entangled in the Con-Textual assemblage. However, this does not hinder the emergence of other kinds of being when they are engaged with other assemblages: e.g. architect's associations, ceramic traditions, academic institutions.

To deconstruct the Islamic being, however, cannot lead to the disenfranchisement of Muslims in the scholarly enquiry. The claim to a flat ontology about decentering humans aims to expand the interests of research to marginalized areas of existence, human and non-human alike. Muslims and Islamized people – Islamic beings – in the present and in the past have been relegated in scholarly practice as a result of the Orientalist complex described by Edward Said (1978) and resituating our interest in them is a vital aspect of decolonization. To focus on assemblages and relationships with things within Islamic archaeology cannot mean to make the role of Islamic human beings to disappear, much less under the pretence of a posthumanist perspective that hides an attempt to make reality uniformly subordinated to Eurocentric knowledge (precisely the kind of fallacy that flat ontology ultimately confronts). To use Deleuzean philosophy in a way that flattens the phenomena of Islam to a reductive perspective merely interested in *explaining* them to a non-Islamic public, would be to fall into a new form of Orientalism.[10] The thing to remember here is that Deleuzean theory should enable mutual understanding, and that requires a particular attention to multivocality and awareness of the position from which scholarship is practiced. From this perspective, Islamic (human) beings should always be present in any conversation about Islam, even if the focus is centred somewhere else. And in any case, the concern of Ahmed about meaning and hermeneutics does not need to be lost in the theory of the assemblages, where expressive aspects are as important as material ones (Crellin 2020: 167; Hamilakis 2017: 172–3; Harris 2018: 89–92). Islamic (human) beings do not need to be ignored, but simply need to be understood as formed as much in the expressive as in the material aspects of the assemblages. Islam is, after all, a form of being human, in the words of Cantwell Smith (1981: 12; see also Chapter 3).

Although the application of Deleuzean theory to the question of Islamic beings is based on radical metaphysics, it should be noted that it does not alter substantially the position that I have been maintaining in this book about the need to consider the historicity of the concept of humanity and its bearing on the question of Islamization. As noted above, Islamization is not only a matter of conversion or cultural assimilation. It must be traced in the flux of relationships that are present in the assemblage of Islamic Con-Text.

Time, change and Islamization

One important consequence of thinking in terms of Deleuzean assemblages is that the concept of time changes completely. Time can no longer be considered as a linear and progressive dimension, empty in itself so that it can be filled up with events. Instead, time emerges from the process of continuous generation of the assemblages. Assemblages are in constant flux, changing every time, although at different rhythms and tempos. These rhythms affect not only the assemblages, but also their elements, so that changes are happening in multiple areas, in diverse ways and in ever different ranges of scales, from the smaller to the larger. This is why Deleuze and Guattari noted that assemblages are continuously becoming (cf. Crellin 2020).

An analysis of Islamization with this concept of time cannot simply aim to conceive the process as the transition between a non- (pre-) Islamic moment to a fully Islamic one. Equally, it cannot be understood as a progressive transformation, from less Islamic to more Islamic. In its purest sense, Islamization would be the becoming of assemblages enfolded by the Islamic Con-Text assemblage. To put it in a different way, Islamization will be the result of a process of territorialization within assemblages that are stratified over the Con-Text. Within each one of these assemblages, Islamization can be perceived of as a process of creation of Con-Text (including Islamic beings, in the sense of conversion *and* of acculturation). From the perspective of the great substratum of the Islamic Con-Text assemblage, Islamization of these overlying assemblages represents only different scales of territorialization and coding.

To make this definition operative in archaeological terms, therefore, we need to consider the issue of scale (Harris 2017; 2018). It is intuitive to think of scale in geographical or historical terms. After all, it is not the same to consider a twenty-year or a 200-year period, or to consider a town or a vast territorial empire. In assemblage theory, however, the scale determines the assemblages under consideration, as well as the strata enfolding them. As assemblages are constantly becoming, the setting of a scale will configure a particular set of enfolded assemblages, with specific relationships, lines of flight and structures that determine parts that are stable (territorialized, coded) and parts that are changing more rapidly (deterritorialized, decoded) (cf. Jervis 2018: 65–8.). Equally, Islamization must take into account what is actual, differenciated, and what is virtual, differentiated (Harris 2021: 54–5). In general, we can assume that a movement from the virtual to the actual defines lines of flight, or processes of territorialization, that inform about the particular process of Islamization in each assemblage. Moving to a different scale will not change those relationships, but it will place them on a different assemblage and enfolding, potentially transforming the meaning of the concepts of change and stability themselves. After all, the sense of 'how long things should last' is different for each being: a mountain can endure eons, while a building can only aspire to endure for a few centuries usually. In a scale appropriate to Islamic things, a mosque emerges from relationships (a building, a place, the people around) that make it last considerably longer than a glazed vessel. What rapid change and stability are turns out differently if we consider separately the mosque and the vessel, but they all exist together.[11]

This does not mean that change cannot be the subject of research. Unilineal and univocal change is out of the question as soon as the concept of time as an empty drawer always moving forward is abandoned. 'Change is messy, complex and multiple' (Crellin 2020: 224), and that is precisely what in Islam allows the meaningful disagreement that Ahmed presents. However, when tracing lines of flight, processes of territorialization and deterritorialization in different assemblages, it is possible to study particular trajectories of change. Crellin (2020: 173–5) advocates to use the concept of phase transition developed by Manuel DeLanda (2006) in this endeavour. The concept of phase transition avoids drawing a hard line, a divergence point in what is otherwise a marked transformation. The example given is the evaporation of water: this is not a sudden change, but a phased one: not all molecules of a body of water reach the boiling point at the same time, and so there is a smooth transition between the two, allowing for a coexistence of the two states of water.[12] The concept of phase transition applied to societies allows for the coexistence of different phases at the same time. We have seen above how Eaton (1993) and Insoll (2003; 2016) preferred the concept of phase to that of period in their consideration of Islamization precisely for this reason (see Chapter 2). The only point of objection that can be made to their conception is the progressive development that the tripartite scheme coexistence-identification-displacement betrays. Another advantage of phase transition is that it overcomes the need for teleological conceptions. Phases are not stages in a pre-determined development, but they indicate the direction of change. The phases described by Eaton and Insoll are very useful in expressing patterns of material changes, but they are too easily read as imposing (rather than indicating) a direction of change – non-Islamic to partially Islamic and partially Islamic to fully Islamic. It would be more coherent with Ahmed's 'meaningful disagreement' to think of these phases as something that reflects the wider connections of the Islamic Con-Text assemblage with other assemblages. After all, all three phases include coexistence of different forms of Islam.

Conclusion: Towards a new perspective of Islamization

In this chapter I have set the stage for a different conception of Islam and Islamization, still based on the ideas of Ahmed, but taking them forward with current archaeological theory. I have used new materialist and posthumanist perspectives, but above all I have worked with Deleuzean metaphysics and the concept of assemblages to lay a different perspective on the matter. If we consider Con-Textual meaning as an assemblage, we can use it as a substratum where other assemblages of Islamic beings (humans and non-humans) can be mapped. The study of Islamization in this perspective becomes an exercise of tracing lines of flight and determining what is differen*t*iated and what is differen*c*iated. In the next chapter I propose two case studies to clarify this idea.

5

Islamization of Communities
Two Case Studies in Early Islam

Introduction: Islamic communities of humans and non-humans

In this chapter I am going to present two case studies of the Islamization of communities composed of humans and non-humans alike. As explained in the previous chapter, I make special mention of the presence of (Islamic) humans to make a smoother connection between Ahmed's work and Deleuzean metaphysics, and to acknowledge the centrality of the question of humanness in Islam. This is not strictly necessary from a purist assemblage theory perspective: all Islamic beings are produced in the same assemblages overlying the Islamic Con-Textual substratum.

The case studies chosen are based on my own research experience and reflect areas where I have expertise rather than being a representative selection of ideal examples. This accounts for the choice of two case studies in the early Islamic period and on areas (Qatar and Iberia) that were conquered during the first (military) Islamic expansion. There is no reason for which the perspectives that I hold in this work cannot be applied to different periods (i.e. later, in the Middle or Late Islamic period, or in the present) or in different territories (e.g. in Sub-Saharan Africa or in the Indian Ocean, vast areas that were rarely incorporated into the Islamic world by military conquest). That does not mean that my case studies are homogenous or even equivalent. They deal with very different geographical areas and trajectories in history.

One common point, however, that can definitely be raised in the two cases of the early Islamic period, is the relationship between the expansion of Islam and a model of existence where (relatively) robust states, urban living, high connectivity (usually represented with links to long distance trade) and a cosmopolitan elite culture are key features. For simplicity in this chapter, I will term this the *Islamicate model of Islamization*, a clear reference to Marshall Hodgson's work, although I am far from supporting his Islamicate-Islamic dichotomy. Some of the main works representative of the model have been presented in Chapter 2, in the analysis of the proposals of Richard Bulliet and Manuel Acién.[1] Research on the available evidence supports much of the narrative that the Islamicate model of Islamization has built around these four themes: state, cities, trade and cosmopolitanism. However, we have seen in the criticism raised in previous chapters that this narrative does not tell the whole story and leaves outside many relevant phenomena of Islam and its Con-Text. In the text that follows I am going to explain how the Islamicate model is present in current research in the areas under consideration, and how the alternative perspective that I am proposing can reinvigorate debate and be inclusive of some forms of Islamization that currently fall outside the model.

Islamization in the Vega of Granada (South East al-Andalus)

Al-Andalus is the name given to the Islamic territory that at its largest extent covered most of the Iberian Peninsula, the Balearic Islands and parts of South France. Its incorporation into the early Islamic-period polity was fast (711–714), in the context of one of the last waves of expansion of the Umayyad Caliphate. It was for some forty years a dependency of the Islamic province of Ifrīqiyya (roughly all of North Africa except Egypt). After the overthrow of the Umayyad dynasty of Damascus by the Abbasids (750), al-Andalus became independent in practice under a branch of the Umayyads, first as an emirate (754–927) and then as a caliphate (927–1032). This second Umayyad Caliphate collapsed in the eleventh century, but al-Andalus continued existing as a highly urbanized society under different political forms. There were up to three periods where it was composed of a mosaic of independent states (Taifa kingdoms) interspersed between the absorption of the territory by the Almoravid (1040–1147) and Almohad Empires (1147–1269) of the Maghrib. The last phase of al-Andalus was represented by the Nasrid Sultanate of Granada (1232–1492), which expanded over the last Islamic territories of the southeast peninsula (all the rest had been progressively lost to the Christian states of the north), up to 1492. The Muslim presence in Iberia did not finish there, however, as many of them continued living for more than a century in different parts of the Peninsula as *Moriscos*, until they were forcefully expelled between 1609 and 1619. In the next section I am going to discuss the Islamization of the core area of Granada, precisely the capital of the last Islamic state of Iberia, but long before it was so. My argument focuses on the period between the eighth and the eleventh centuries.

The Vega of Granada: A linear approach to Islamization (c. 711–1090)

The Vega of Granada is a basin between the southeast mountains of Iberia (the Sub-Baetic system) where the River Genil creates a fertile area. The Vega itself is an area with a roughly triangular shape, 40 km long and between 3 and 9 km wide. It can be divided into two distinct areas: a more humid, wider one, to the east (from where the river comes down from the Sierra Nevada mountains); and another one, drier and less extensive, to the west (where the water leaves the eastern part). The two main towns of the area, Ilbīra and Granada, were in the eastern side. Granada is the place of the Roman town of Iliberis, and Ilbīra seems to have been founded at some point between the sixth and the ninth centuries. Ilbīra was the capital of the Vega, and of a more extensive region (a *kūra*, or province) up to the eleventh century, when it was abandoned, and the capital was moved to Granada. The western side did not have a town until the end of the ninth century, when Loja was founded (Figure 5.1).

Figure 5.1 Map of the Vega of Granada, showing the towns in the region in the early Islamic period. Map elaborated by Jorge Rouco Collazo.

The foundation of towns and the expansion of the urban world were distinctive traits of the early Islamic period in the Vega of Granada (and in other regions of al-Andalus). Towns became associated with a better integration of the territory of the Vega (and of the whole province) in the structure of the Umayyad state of Cordoba. This was not only about political submission to Cordoba: it was a true social transformation. It created a new economic and cultural elite that, in turn, was more than ever dependent on trade circuits and on the state resources to keep them open and viable. The verification of all these points in different parts of al-Andalus by Manuel Acién became the basis of his theoretical approach (explained in Chapter 2), and of the Islamicate model of Islamization. In Acién's view, Islamization takes the form of a *transition* between the pre-Islamic and the Islamic society. The transition is completed when the society becomes fully integrated in the Umayyad state. Although the social transformations on which the Islamicate model is based are well supported by evidence, the unilinearity and steadiness of the process described by Acién can be questioned.

The transformation has been documented in changes in the archaeological record in the Vega of Granada (Table 5.1). The Muslims arrived in the Vega around 712 (one year after the start of the Islamic conquest of al-Andalus in 711), in one of the first expeditions to take over the peninsula, and initiated a transformation that can be structured in four phases (Carvajal López 2008; 2009; 2022; forthcoming; Carvajal López and Day 2013). In Phase I of this development (*c.* 550–*c.* 800),[2] the material culture retained many traits of the previous centuries, but new ceramic forms and technologies were introduced and new settlements were founded. The new sites reflected the exploitation of new economic niches (thanks to the installation of irrigation systems). The evidence suggests that the production of ceramics is distributed in several archaeological sites in the Vega.

In Phase II (*c.* 800–925), the range of pottery techniques and forms increased, as did the number of productive centres of ceramics. Although ceramics were made in different places, the now fully functioning towns of Ilbīra and Granada had a central role in production and distribution. There is written evidence of the high productivity of irrigation fields at this point (Jiménez Puertas and Carvajal López 2011), although they had yet to reach a wider extension and more importance in the economy of the region. This was a period of unrest, as the proliferation of fortifications shows, but it was also a period when contacts with other regions were attested (ceramics from the Middle East and North Africa have been found in the region: see Carvajal López 2008: 287; Salinas Pleguezuelo et al 2019: 11). On the political side, the Umayyad state of Cordoba began to assert more effectively its presence and influence in the region. For example, the Umayyads founded the first mosque of the town of Ilbīra in 864 (perhaps in the same place where a previous mosque had been founded, but this is not confirmed archaeologically) and they became actively involved in the disputes over the control of the region between different factions in the area (Carvajal López 2013).

Table 5.1 Table showing the phases of development of Islamization of the Vega of Granada

Phase	Dates		Comment
Phase I	c. 550–c. 800	Phase Ia c.550–c. 711	Development of a distinctive late antique tradition of ceramic production. From Phase Ib, introduction of new forms and techniques and opening of new economic niches by Muslim conquerors.
		Phase Ib c. 711–c. 800	
Phase II	c. 800–c. 925		Documentation of irrigation fields and of fortifications, conflicts with the Umayyad state of Cordoba. Contact between different sites and with distant places, in al-Andalus and beyond. In ceramics, there is an accumulation of technological innovation. A range of technical solutions for the same types of vessels is observed.
Phase III	c. 925–c. 1011		Caliphal period, zenith of the town of Ilbira. Abandonment of many rural sites and concentration of population in the capital. Concentration of ceramic workshops in the town of Ilbira. This leads to homogeneity of technical solutions and forms.
Phase IV	c. 1011–c. 1150		End of the Caliphate of Cordoba and foundation of the Zirid state of Granada, followed by Almoravid conquest. Abandonment of Ilbira and relocation of the population to Granada. Ceramic workshops move to the new capital. Technical conditions remain largely the same, despite new typologies.

Phase III (c. 925–1011) was the golden age of the town of Ilbīra, when the power of the Umayyad state had gained a strong foothold in the region (and in fact, was a well-established and recognized power in the Mediterranean, as its transformation in Caliphate in 927 shows). The ceramic production of the Vega seems to have been concentrated in the towns (local ceramics forms are made only in Granada or in Ilbīra) and the range of techniques and forms of vessels was standardized (and therefore the number of types was reduced). Trade flourished, as the number of imports shows (most of them probably came from Almeria, the main port of the Caliphate). Irrigated agriculture was the central economic activity, as it provided the food necessary for the large urban population and its taxation produced high revenues for the state. The urban phenomenon was well consolidated at this point. In fact, the urban world survived and thrived in the following phase, despite the collapse of the Umayyad state (cf. López Martínez de Marigorta 2020: Chapters 2 and 4).

The change to Phase IV (c. 1011 to 1150)[3] was precipitated by the end of Umayyad authority in the Vega. The town of Ilbīra was sacked by Berbers (former military retinues of the Umayyad government) and the Zirid dynasty (another Berber tribe) took over. The Zirids founded a new state and moved the capital to the town of Granada. This movement is well documented in the archaeological record: the workshops of Ilbīra disappeared and were relocated to Granada. In this town there was an expansion of the fortified space and an increase in the number of mosques. Its territory saw a fast development of irrigated spaces, and the toponyms associated to these suggest that some of them could have been privatized. The pottery produced in Granada was being consumed in large amounts in other villages of the Vega. This was the last step to complete the process of transformation by which the urban sphere became the centre of Andalusi society, at least in the Vega of Granada. The urban hegemony was not possible without the support of the state apparatus (in this case Zirid, not Umayyad), as well as the sustainability offered by irrigated agriculture and the trade networks that fed the luxury items that allowed certain cultural and economic elites to distinguish themselves (cf. López Martínez de Marigorta 2020: Chapters 6 and 7; Sarr Marrocco 2011).

This is an overview of changes appreciated in the Vega of Granada between the eighth and the eleventh century, and that *could* be presented as the process of Islamization if one adopts Acién's perspective. However, although this succession of events and phenomena is supported by evidence, I believe that it would be a mistake to adopt it as the only possible path of Islamization, for the reasons that I develop in the next section.

Islamization in the Vega of Granada: A critique and an alternative

The problem with the Islamicate narrative presented above is that it threads together a number of well-evidenced phenomena in a story where the progression towards the society of the Umayyad (and Zirid) state is conflated with Islamization. However, as I have explained above, Islamization is a lot more than that. It is about the creation and expansion of Con-Text. It certainly cannot be denied that the establishment and development of the Umayyad (and then Zirid) state is a form of Con-Textual growth. But there were other forms too, and in some cases these alternative forms presented direct contradiction with the Con-Textual expansion on which the state supported its own existence by fostering alternative ways of being and becoming Islamic. In other words, the main problem with the Islamicate model of Islamization is that it leaves no space for alternative Con-Textual constructions.

As we have seen in the section above, an archaeological survey of the Vega of Granada in the crucial centuries of the early Islamic period shows an abundant number of transformations happening at the same time. Besides the urban expansion, there are significant social changes; important rearrangements in the organization of the settlement patterns of the Vega; the development and growth in extension and complexity of the irrigation systems; and, last but not least, a wave of innovation in ceramic technology and distribution. In the theory of Islamization of Acién, all these aspects are made to be aligned with the becoming of the Umayyad state of Cordoba. There is no doubt that the processes that generated and were generated by the exercise and expansion of the political power of the Umayyad state of Cordoba had an impact on the lives and trajectories of beings – human and not human – in the Vega of Granada. However, if we accept that Islamic beings generate Con-Text and are in turn becoming as part of that Con-Text, then it follows that the Umayyad state cannot be considered the only agent of change. Rather, change and agency need to be distributed along different beings and relationships to generate significant Con-Text and therefore Islamization. This is where the consideration of assemblage theory becomes useful.

In Chapter 4, I explained how we can discuss Islamization with the help of the concept of Deleuzean assemblages. In order to achieve this, we need to abandon the unilineal concept of time as an empty structure and embrace the habit of thinking of different scales, assemblages and enfolded strata. The different strata under consideration are assemblages that expand over a range of scales and dimensions. These dimensions include elements of the 'hard' physical world, such as things, people and places, but also the interrelations between them, which involve symbols, feelings, meanings, etc. The selection of a particular scale, in our case that of the Vega of Granada in the early Islamic period (eighth to eleventh centuries), allows us to focus our attention on a particular region of all these assemblages, where they enfold and become enfolded in unique ways. Therefore, we can study the Con-Text *in loco* of the early Islamic Vega of Granada as a particular region of the Islamic Con-Textual assemblage that is uniquely stratified and enfolded by a number of different assemblages in contact. Our work as archaeologists is to understand how these different assemblages connect to each other, and how far we can learn about the Islamic Con-Text by mapping the assemblages that enfold it.

One way to understand the connection between assemblages is to analyze (that is, to map) the connection between territorialization and deterritorialization of some assemblages and the coding and decoding of others, as this is where strata touch each other. The analysis of the movement of beings between virtuality and actuality allows us to explore these assemblages, as this movement goes along the lines of flight that define them. The issue of scale is at play here once again. Beings emerge out of assemblages as combinations of different elements, but our selection of scale can determine how far we are able to move along the lines of flight of a given assemblage. Therefore, our scale selection involves also choosing the beings that we are going to study. For example, the aim of our enquiry in this case study is not the whole dimension of the concept (assemblage) of Human Being, as clearly its trajectory escapes by far from the scope of our scale; we are rather focusing on the Islamic human being, a different assemblage stratified over that of the Human Being. Equally, we are not interested in the long history of the Geographical Vega of Granada, a region with characteristic historical, geological and environmental features. Our early Islamic-period Vega of Granada is in itself a stratified assemblage over the Geographical Vega of Granada. It is important to understand that our selection of scale does not involve only a focus on a particular region of a wider assemblage; it actually involves the creation of beings (the becoming of new assemblages) by enclosing the relationships between particular sets of elements under a specific enquiry. This, in turn, determines conditions of virtuality and actuality.

In the next section I am going to apply these theoretical ideas by focusing on particular assemblages centred around very specific Islamic beings: ceramic vessels. By understanding the assemblages on which these ceramic vessels become virtual or actual, I will try to understand how an assemblage of Islamic ceramic vessels becomes. In other words, I am going to discuss the Islamization of different ceramic vessels in the early Islamic-period Vega of Granada.

The Islamization of cooking pots and large containers in the Vega of Granada[4]

In this section I am going to analyze the transformations in ceramic vessels between the eighth and eleventh centuries, with some observations going a bit beyond these limits (so that changes can be understood

Islamization of Communities: Two Case Studies in Early Islam 103

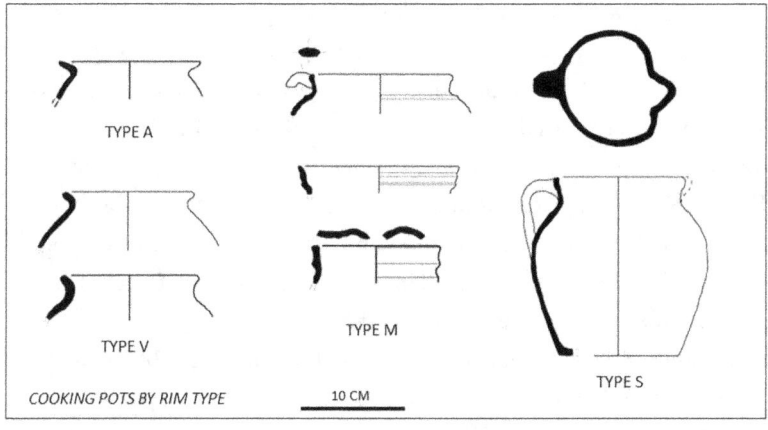

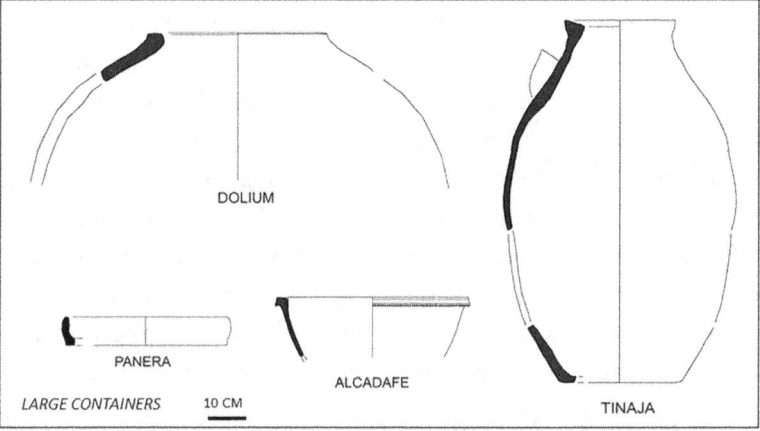

Figure 5.2 Ceramic types from the Vega of Granada discussed in this chapter. The scale is indicative, as sizes are variable within a range. Elaborated by the author.

better). I am going to focus on two particular assemblages: cooking pots and large containers (Figure 5.2). The aim is to map these assemblages and to understand their relationship with Islamic Con-Text.

The cooking pots on which I am focusing are relatively small vessels with globular shape and a capacity of between 2 and 3 litres. They were normally made in a fabric of brown to black colour (very frequently red or orange), with abundant inclusions of quartzitic rocks (usually phyllite, schist or quartzite) and a range of other metamorphic and sedimentary minerals and rocks. Another aspect that these vessels shared is the territorial dispersion of their networks of production and distribution. These vessel types are very characteristic of the area of the Vega of Granada. Moving to nearby regions, such as the Campiña of Jaen or the Coast of Granada, one can find completely new typological ranges of vessels used for the same function (cf. respectively Castillo Armenteros 1998; Gómez Becerra 1998).

An analysis of the changes in cooking pots can begin by looking at a typology based on their rims. The rims of the pots made in pre-Islamic periods are Types A and V, and from the eighth century we find Types S and M. The difference between the two pairs goes beyond morphology: the rim types introduced in the Islamic period were higher and more clearly separated from the neck, so that they could be shaped to create a beaker without affecting the globular body. This suggests that at least some vessels of the 'new' Type S and M cooking pots were designed to pour liquid on a different container, and therefore there were functional differences as well. Type A vessels disappeared probably in the eighth century (if not before), but V-type vessels continued to be made, albeit more rarely, until the ninth century at least. Type M, and specially Type S cooking pots were predominant after the eighth century. From the tenth century onwards new cooking pots were made in the towns of Ilbīra and Granada (Types E and I) and they largely substituted Types S and M.

The technology of production of cooking pots changed quite substantially from the tenth century onwards. All the data suggests that the production was concentrated in the urban workshops of Ilbīra first and of Granada afterwards. There was an important move to standardization then. This can be seen in a relatively reduced typological range of cooking pots (Types E and I are predominant, but are not the only ones), but it is even clearer in the decrease of technological variability at large. The range of techniques available to potters to make cooking pots was wider before the tenth century, before the workshops were concentrated in the towns. This wider technological variability was very characteristic of the earliest Islamic period in the Vega of Granada, the eighth and ninth centuries, but it is not seen before the Islamic conquest. An analysis of the pre-Islamic-period patterns of cooking pot production shows that the technological range was probably even narrower than in the tenth century.

So, it is worth narrowing the scale of our mapping of the cooking pot assemblage to the period between the eighth and the ninth centuries. As noted above, this is the moment where Types S and M were predominant in the Vega of Granada, but this typological predominance is not reflected in the range of techniques used to produce the pots: the same morphological types could be made with different techniques. In fact, a large part of the innovations detected in the eighth and ninth centuries are not specifically typological but are mostly in the realm of technology. I have noted above how the change in the morphology of the rims made it possible to add beakers to the design of the cooking pots. Other technological changes involved wheeling techniques: the walls of the cooking pots after the eighth century tend to be thinner, which suggests a higher speed of the wheel and a different know-how on the part of the potter. From the ninth century at least, a different way of finishing the bases of the cooking pots is documented in some sites of the Vega of Granada (not in all of them, and that is relevant as well, as will be noted below). Before the ninth century, all the cooking pots used to have a flat base with marks left by the wire used to separate the vessel from the wheel. The new finishing technique involved the scraping (and sometimes the cutting) of the base of the pot to give it a convex sagging profile. This was an additional operation that required a different way of wheeling the pot (the base had to be a bit thicker to endure the scraping) and the ability of the potter to manipulate the vessel when it was bone dry. The resulting convex base had some advantages in the transmission of temperature (Fernández Navarro 2008: 172) and in its stability over irregular surfaces (Arthur 2007: 179), but it is not at all sure if this technological introduction was only because of functionality: it is likely a way to contribute to the materialization of traits of identification of a community with particular ways of making and using cooking pots (Carvajal López and Jiménez Puertas 2017: 42–3; cf. similar cases in Gosselain 1998; 2000; 2008; 2010; Mahias 1993). Finally, potters experimented with different clay recipes to produce their cooking pots. From the ninth century onwards (perhaps as early as the eighth century), potters created new clay recipes to make use of raw materials within reach of their workshops and at the same time good performance (involving, in this case, the ability to withstand thermal shock and to transmit heat). They seem to have been able to find successful recipes in each workshop (and in some cases, more than one recipe). It is very clear, however, that they were not ignoring the previous ceramic traditions. The potters of the Islamic period took and used the know-how of the potters that preceded them. This indicates a degree of communication among different communities; in some cases, the recipes used before the Islamic period were maintained at the same time that new recipes were created. Therefore, there is an extraordinary range of technological variety in cooking pot production in the ninth century in the Vega of Granada that disappeared when the production was concentrated in urban workshops in the tenth century.

Before analyzing the case of the cooking pots in more detail, it is worth looking at the assemblage of large containers, where much of the same happens with certain particularities. The large containers are vessels usually too large to have been made in a wheel, although in some cases parts of them could be manufactured in this way. Unlike the cooking pots, they do not include a single type of vessel. In this category I have included the Roman *dolia* and the Islamic-period *tinajas*, used mainly for storage and less likely for transport of liquids and other goods. The *paneras* are basins of thick walls used for cooking bread, documented in North Africa and Iberia since Antiquity and up to the Islamic period (and are still produced in parts of North Africa nowadays). Similar to these are the Islamic-period *alcadafes*, basins that in al-Andalus have been associated with domestic chores and in the Middle East with wine and oil production (cf. Abu Aemar and Carvajal López 2014; Magness 1993).[5] The *dolia* and the *paneras* documented in the Vega of Granada clearly came from the pre-Islamic period, and they were still used in the eighth century. It is likely, however, that the *dolia* were no longer being produced then, and, in fact, they disappeared from the archaeological record. The *paneras* were produced perhaps for a bit longer, but they also vanished around the ninth century. It is clear that the *tinajas* and *alcadafes* were introduced in al-Andalus in the eighth century and have continued being part of any ceramic assemblage until today.

The technological aspects of this assemblage of large containers are very interesting. There is clearly an overlap of functions between *dolia* and *tinajas*, which would explain in part the disappearance of the former. However, there are important differences. The *dolia* were designed as architectural fixings, and therefore were extremely large and were not designed to be moved around. Their ceramic fabric was very dense, featuring very small inclusions or even a very purified clay. The *tinajas* were large as well, but smaller and not so usually fixed (although spaces for them could be carved in houses). It is very likely that *tinajas* occupied an intermediate space in between the functions of the *dolia* and those of the amphorae: so, they had to be sturdy and solid enough to store goods, but they could also be loaded in animals or carts to be used as transport. The ceramic fabric used for the manufacture of the *tinajas* was very different to that of the *dolia*: it contained large inclusions (of the same geological background as that of the cooking pots) that produced a ceramic fabric with abundant micro-cracks, useful to reduce the overall weight of the vessel and to give it more porosity and resistance to stress. It was, therefore, a fabric that could withstand a certain amount of stress because of changing conditions of pressure, humidity and temperature, but which was also light enough to be moved around. It is interesting to note here that the potters who designed the fabrics for the *tinajas* found inspiration in the fabric used for the *paneras* (designed to withstand thermal stress) and ignored any precedents from the *dolia*. But they also experimented with new recipes and introduced grog and calcareous rocks as ways to produce even lighter vessels. As in the case of the cooking pots, the production of *tinajas* shows wide technological variability during the ninth century and standardization from the tenth century onwards.

The *alcadafes* mark another interesting innovation. Although they seem morphologically closer to the *paneras*, their uses were wider. The main innovation introduced by the *alcadafe* was the ability to shift workspaces: they were basically mobile basins with a large capacity, so they could be moved around a house (or group of houses) or even across different campsites to establish flexible spaces for different types of work. They could be used in a domestic or an industrial sphere. As they shared the requisite of mobility with the *tinajas*, they were made with the same kind of fabrics.

It is therefore fair to say that there are many shared features between the assemblage of the large containers and that of the cooking pots, mapped above. In both cases there was a period of technological innovation that started with the Islamic conquest of the Vega of Granada and lasted until around the beginning of the tenth century. This innovation was manifested in an expansion of the range of techniques available to the potters in different segments of the production process, which I will term *technological dispersion*. From the tenth century onwards, the production of ceramic vessels became concentrated around towns and the technology of production underwent standardization, therefore narrowing down the range of techniques of production available. This process will be labelled *technological coalescence*.

Let us focus for a moment on the second part of this progression, the coalescence of technologies after the start of the tenth century. This may well be the result of a process of demographic concentration in towns and readjustment of the work division. However, there is written evidence to suggest that the methodology of pottery production in towns such as Granada and Ilbīra was regulated by legal contracts between potters and wholesalers, suggesting some level of state and law involvement in this system.[6] This supports to a large extent the Islamicate vision of Islamization, where the development of the Umayyad state and towns is equated with the advance of Islamization. This can be accepted as a form of Con-Textual expansion, but it would be a mistake to consider it the only one. It is therefore necessary to find alternative engagements with Con-Text. For this reason, it is worth considering the assemblages of cooking pots and large containers before the tenth century, when the influence of the Umayyad state and the towns is much more reduced (and therefore the stratification of the assemblages is different). We can see then that the dispersion and coalescence of technology are not necessarily exclusive of each other.

As noted above, the period between the eighth and ninth centuries was one of innovation and technological dispersion. This was certainly not the result of the work of a single or even localized group of craftspeople, because the different innovative trends were localized in different sites and periods across the Vega of Granada between the eighth and the ninth century. In part, this was probably the result of the arrival of different groups of immigrants, each one bringing in different traditions of pottery making that were adapted in different ways and were reproduced in different segments of the *chaîne opératoire*, generating entirely new sequences of techniques. But the arrival of immigrants cannot be treated as a black box to explain changes. In fact, the act of innovation, that is, how a particular technique came to be in al-Andalus, is entirely a secondary question in this discussion. What is relevant is to understand the conditions and the timing under which new and old techniques were adopted, adapted and recombined to generate new processes of production, and the meanings that accompanied these. Further studies need to be made to reach that aim, but it is possible to explore some relevant ideas.

Between the eighth and ninth centuries, the Vega of Granada was a mosaic of different communities with their own pottery workshops, but they were not unrelated to each other. It is interesting to note that they shared the same notion of types of vessels, and even of the typologies of cooking pots; this means that, even when using different *chaînes opératoires*, their products were clearly recognizable between themselves: they all produced cooking pots of the Types S and M, *tinajas* and *alcadafes*. They also had a common conception of how a vessel should be when a range of options were available. To put it in Deleuzean terms, not only they differenciated (produced the actual) the same pots, but they also differentiated (produced the virtual, conceived their best possible design) them in the same way. This can be seen in the fact that innovative techniques coalesce together: the new wheeling techniques, the new fabrics, are applied to the Type S and Type M cooking pots, but not to the Types A or V. They were applied to *tinajas* and *alcadafes*, but not to *dolia* or *paneras*. Therefore, there were co-existing trends in the technological developments of the assemblages in consideration: a tendency to technological dispersion and to making innovations coalesce in one particular direction. Coming back to the language of assemblage theory: these trends of dispersion and coalescence are equivalent to directions of lines of flight of our assemblages. The assemblages deterritorialize towards the direction of technological dispersion and territorialize towards coalescence.

Assemblages also have structures and codes related to their lines of flight. The codes in this case are the meanings associated with dispersion and coalescence of technology. Where technology disperses, there is decoding: the meanings are broken down because they cannot be used to account for the range of phenomena observed. This is represented by the abandonment of certain lines of development of technology: *dolia*, *paneras* and Types A and V cooking pots stopped being made between the eighth and the ninth centuries. But with decoding comes coding: the search for new meanings to make sense of the new reality. The coalescence of technologies in the new shapes and *chaînes opératoires* is not only craftsmanship but is also an act of identity in the sense that it cements a particular conception of the world and of the beings and relationships that compose it.

From this perspective, it is possible to understand the process of standardization and narrowing down of technological options of the tenth century in a new light. The aim here is not to reject the relevance of the role of the state, of the towns and of the demographic concentration in them. These phenomena are all there, as strata enfolding the assemblages of the cooking pots and large containers, and contributing, in part, with a measure of their own agency. However, the mapping of these assemblages allows us to see the disappearance of some of the technical innovations introduced only one century before, and the selection and concentration of some other techniques as acts of creation of meaning to make sense of particular circumstances of life.

To summarize the process above, between the eighth and the eleventh centuries in the Vega of Granada we can see how different strata (assemblages) enfold the assemblages of the cooking pots and of the large containers, establishing the lines of flight over which technological dispersion and coalescence (deterritorialization and territorialization, decoding and coding respectively, unfold). The assemblages in question point towards instances of creation or abandoning of meaning that necessarily connect with other assemblages, as they go beyond cooking pots and large containers themselves. Cooking pots are connected with ways of preparing and serving food; *tinajas* and *alcadafes* reflect ideas on when and how to store and use water, liquids or other elements in domestic and industrial contexts; and the production of all ceramic vessels is related to ways of understanding the 'proper way' to do technological operations. All these ideas are at the same time connected to wider concepts of identity, appropriateness, sociality, cosmology, etc. Whenever we think of the meaning of a particular assemblage or element of assemblages, we are drawn to new relationships and to new assemblages. This is an effect of the enfolding of assemblages: when properly considered, things cannot simply stand on their own *thingness*. They are all connected to other things in vertiginous relationships that reach immeasurable depths. These connections reach, of course, the Islamic Con-Textual assemblage. In this sense, all the transformations described so far speak about the Islamization of cooking pots and large containers.

The key process to understand how Islamization and these transformations are connected by deep connection of meanings, is the enfolding or stratification of assemblages. In the next section, I take my focus off of the assemblages of the ceramic vessels and target Islamic Con-Text once again.

Islamic Con-Text as substratum

In the formulation of Ahmed, Con-Text is a vocabulary of meanings. But meaning does not, cannot, exist as a purely intellectual concept: it is linked to a structure of relationships and things, to an assemblage in itself. In a Deleuzean formulation, Con-Text can be defined as a substratum, an assemblage enfolding the creation of meaning in Islamic societies. It territorializes where the meaning of being Islamic becomes clear and distinct, and deterritorializes where the meaning blurs. It therefore models the coding and decoding structures for the assemblages that stratify over it. In other words, it provides the 'blueprints' of the production of Islamic beings at a particular scale, whether these are human or not human. A Muslim (Islamic being) emerges out of a Con-Textual assemblage. An Islamic cooking pot (another Islamic being) has exactly the same origin.

But we cannot be misled by the label 'substratum' and conceive Islamic Con-Text as a monolithic and unchangeable level that gives shape to everything that it enfolds. In Deleuzean metaphysics, a substratum is another assemblage, and it is as liable to change (to scale-bounded territorialization and deterritorialization) as any of the strata above and below. From an assemblage-internal perspective, this is perceived as a continuous creation and modification of Con-Text as time moves forward, but from an external perspective, time itself is the result of the trajectory of the lines of flight of the assemblage contemplated at a given scale.

Mapping the Islamic Con-Text is useful to understand how it enfolds with other assemblages at a particular scale. But it can also be understood in the opposite way. When we wonder about Islamization in a given historical context, the mapping of the assemblages of interest can help us to detect the lines of flight of the Islamic Con-Textual assemblage. There is no point in questioning which aspects of life of a community are affected by Islamization and which ones would have developed equally had Islamization not been there. Islamization enfolds every aspect of life of an Islamic community, and therefore every phenomenon, action and event within that life is bound to be given an Islamic meaning and absorbed into Con-Text. Therefore, every being emerging from an assemblage enfolded by Islamic Con-Text is bound to become an Islamic being.

This is how we know that the cooking pots and large containers in the Vega of Granada between the eighth and the eleventh centuries could be 'Islamized'. They (each one individually, and the assemblages that they form) were the result of a meaning-creation action by other Islamic beings as much as they were materially produced by potters in their workshops. The particular conditions of innovation of these assemblages – technology dispersion and coalescence – show that these acts of meaning-creation would be necessarily frequent too. And not only with regard to cooking pots and large containers. Beyond these assemblages, there were many other instances that are documented where creation of meaning was happening in relation to social and technological innovation. Without abandoning ceramics, there are many other innovations that could be listed in the eighth and ninth centuries: new ceramic forms, such as lamps, chafing dishes, jugs or jars; new decorations, such as different types of glazing, scratching, painting, etc. The well connected networks of trade, both internal and external, of al-Andalus provide abundant objects and relationships that once again require an expansion of meaning. Moving beyond ceramics, the expansion of irrigated agriculture implied the introduction of new work processes, social organizations, crop availability and environmental conditions. Finally, there is no doubt that the arrival of migrants and of new ways of understanding the world, and in general the inclusion of the Iberian peninsula in the Islamic community, also brought the need to understand a completely new world.

These meanings, of course, are not necessarily aligned in the same direction. It is likely that a courtesan in the Umayyad court would have different expectations of Islamization from a tribal leader of the Arabs of the Vega of Granada, in the same way that the perspectives of a male 'alim (religious scholar) would be different from those of a peasant woman. The examples of reasons for disagreement are as many as the different conditions of Islamization. These disagreements (*dispersion*) reflect the influence of diverse enfolded assemblages, but at the same time show the ways in which disagreements can be overcome and agreements reached (*coalescence*). In the case of the Vega of Granada between the eighth and the eleventh centuries, politics seems to have been marked by local coalescence and regional dispersion until the ninth century, with a wider degree of coalescence reached under the Umayyad state around the tenth century.

Islamization in Qatar

For the second case study I will focus on a very different part of the planet: the Qatar peninsula. Qatar is a nation on the Arabian side of the Persian Gulf that occupies a small, flat peninsula and several islands. As a nation it became independent in 1972, but it had a long trajectory of independence that can be traced to at least the nineteenth century, when the Al-Thānī dynasty (current holders of the Emiral dignity and rulers of the country) were recognized as the regional governors of the area, first by the Ottomans and then by the British. The history of Qatar, however, has deep roots and is crucial to understanding the Islamization of the whole area, as recent archaeological research shows.

The Gulf in the Early Islamic Period (c. 622–1000 CE): The Islamicate model

The narrative of Islamization of the Gulf has not been developed in depth in any work, but in general it aligns well with the themes of the Islamicate model. After the Revelation to Muḥammad, the construction and consolidation of an Islamic polity came as the result of the political and military victories of the Prophet and his successors, the Caliphs. The generation of an urban and multicultural society that became the landmark of the Islamic (or the Islamicate) way of life, and the development of connectivity across wide expanses of territory allowed for the mobility of people, goods and ideas at scales that were not possible before. Although the interlocking of the themes is not as clearly laid out as in Acién's theory for al-Andalus, the linear causal relationship between them is quite evident.

The Gulf was included in the first Islamic polity almost since the beginning: Gulf Arabs accepted the message of the Prophet before his death (632) and remained in their majority faithful during the Wars of the Apostasy, or *Riddah* (632–634). During these years, tribes all over Arabia revolted against the successor of Muḥammad, Abū Bakr, but the Gulf remained mostly loyal, with some notable exceptions in Bahrein and Oman (Donner 1981: 82–90; King 1997: 83–5; Serjeant 1978: 149–51). Only a few years later, in 637, the Gulf Arabs were vital in supporting, by sea, the Islamic expansion into the Sassanian Empire. Although the main Muslim force had entered the Sassanian lands via Iraq, by land, a second force of Arabs crossed the Gulf and invaded Iran directly. The campaign culminated with the conquest of Fars in *c.* 648–650, when the two forces reunited (King 1997: 85–6; Whitcomb 1986: 221; cf. al-Balādhurī II 1924: 127–30; al-Ṭabarī XIV 1994: 68–9). The influence of the Gulf Muslims in the Iranian side of the sea was important in the following years. In 680–692 the Second *Fitna* ('period of chaos') of the Caliphate took place, and several anti-Caliphs emerged in opposition to the Umayyad dynasty. In Kirman (Southern Iran), Qaṭarī ibn al-Fujāʾa, a Muslim from Eastern Arabia (maybe from the peninsula of Qatar), became the Caliph elected by the Azraqi Kharijis in 689, until his defeat and death in 691 (EI IV 1997: 752–3). The presence of Arabs in the Iranian coast is not surprising, since the interaction of populations on both sides of the Gulf is historically well attested (see Whitcomb 2009b: 78 and al-Istakhrī 1927: 141 for the early Islamic period; for the modern period, see al-Dailami 2014; Holes 2011; Potter 1998: 127–9; Slot 1993 1–51). However, the fact that an Eastern Arab could lead a rival Caliphate in Iran suggests a stronger presence of groups of Gulf Arabs than usual (Figure 5.3).

The narrative of Islamization of the Gulf, however, is not so much centred around military conquest or the presence of Arabs, but rather in the geographical position of the Gulf as a trade gateway between the

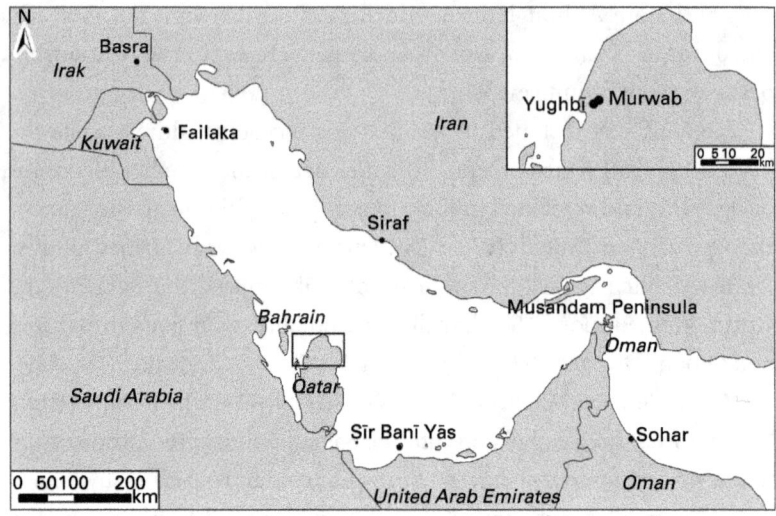

Figure 5.3 Map of the Gulf with indication of the sites discussed in the text. Map elaborated by Jorge Rouco Collazo.

core lands of the Caliphate and the Indian Ocean. By the beginning of the Islamic period, the Gulf had a strong history of connections between the civilizations of Eastern Arabia and the Omani Peninsula with Mesopotamia, India and East Africa (for an overview, see Kennet 2004; Priestman 2021; Tomber 2008). The arrival of Islam would boost the range and intensity of these connections, linking China with the Gulf, with a direct navigation route for the first time in history.[7] At the same time, connectivity in the Gulf was closely related to the development of the urban world, since it was considered to be the force behind the growth of demand that triggered the expansion of trade (Chaudhuri 1985: 51).

Towns and cities are the link between state and trade in the Islamic period. The first urban foundations of Islamic history are always associated with the manifestation of power. The *amṣār* (sg. *miṣr*) were garrison cities for Arab troops in territories that were considered hostile, and they were the very first model of city developed when the Islamic conquest poured out of Arabia (the very first foundations documented are Basra and Kufa in 637 and 638 respectively) (Akbar 1989; Kennedy 2010). In later periods, urban development was linked to state rulers to a large extent, although this was more a manifestation of power than a prerogative. Nowhere is this clearer than in the foundation of dynastic cities all over the territories of the Islamic polity, from the Abbasid cities of Baghdad (762) and Samarra (836) in Iraq or Raqqa (796) in Syria, to the succession of dynastic foundations that formed the conurbation of Cairo in Egypt (Fusṭāṭ was founded as a miṣr in 640, and it was followed by al-ʿAskar in 750, al-Qaṭāʿi in 869 and al-Qāhirah in 969). However, it would be a mistake to place the city exclusively within the sphere of the state. The urban environment was fundamental in allowing the regulation and taxing of trade by the state: cities were the places where aswāq (sg. sūq, 'market') were and where craftsmanship was concentrated. Therefore, the foundation of cities by the state is at the same time an index of the level of trade and of the involvement of the states in the regulation of that trade (ibidem).

This is the crux of the link between the development of trade in the Gulf and the foundation and expansion of cities. A case example here would be Basra. Founded in 637 as a miṣr, it would eventually become the gateway to Baghdad, founded in 762 by the second Abbasid Caliph, al-Manṣūr (r. 754–775). The foundation of Baghdad is traditionally considered the starting point of the period of the highest degree of connectivity of the Gulf. It is certainly true that during the eighth and ninth centuries CE, the main cities involving long-distance trade in the Gulf were founded: Sohar (Oman) at some point in the late-seventh century or early-eighth century (Priestman 2021, I: 126–34, Siraf between 750 and 800 CE (ibidem: 79–90 Whitehouse 2009). The connectivity of the Gulf peaks during this time period, and there is a direct route between Basra and several centres in China, with colonies of merchants of different religions being established there, at least by the mid-eighth century (cf. Carvajal López 2017 for a recent appraisal of sources).

Urban development, however, is not the only impact that the formation of the Islamic polity and trade are considered to have had on demographics. All over the Gulf there is an increase in the archaeological visibility of rural settlements, and this has been interpreted as evidence of a demographic expansion and sedentarization of nomads (cf. Kennet 2012 and all the evidence included thereby). A similar move from nomadism to sedentism is documented in different parts of the Islamic world in its early centuries (e.g. Whitcomb 2009a for Syria) and has been linked to the Islamicate model, either produced under direct state pressure (e.g. Haiman 1995 for the Negev) or because of adaptation to an agricultural model of subsistence (e.g. Avni 2014: 260–83 for the same area).[8] The fact that the nomadic communities of the Gulf are settling down at the same time as cities (linked to the state, as explained above) emerge all over the area could be interpreted in line with the Islamicate model too. In the particular case of Qatar, this association is materialized in the large site of Murwab, formed by clusters of sedentarized or semi-sedentarized communities around a quadrangular fort in its centre (Guérin and Al-Naʿīmī 2009; 2010). The plan of this fortification suggests the presence of some kind of state authority, which could explain why the different communities concentrated there. Therefore, the site of Murwab could, in principle, provide support for the idea of sedentarization at the behest of government administration.

The influence of the Islamicate model in the intellectual perception of Islamization in the Gulf can also be noted in narratives that consider what happened after all the developments registered during the early Islamic period. From the tenth century onwards, a decrease in connectivity is perceived in the Gulf, and this is interpreted as a collapse of the institutions that had been responsible for its rise: state, urban model and sedentism. In the Gulf, the failure of the Abbasid state to pacify Southern Iraq during the Zanj revolt (869–83) and to quell the rise of the Qarmatians in the tenth century is considered a turning point (Kennedy 2014). The Qarmatians are, in turn, considered to be one of the main reasons for stalled connectivity in the Gulf, as they set up high tolls and taxes to trade (Agius 2008: 72; Ibn Hawqāl 1992: 33) and thus indirectly encouraged traders to use the Red Sea route, under the control of the Fatimids of Egypt (Power 2009). Another political event, this time on the other side of the Indian Ocean, is considered to have discouraged direct navigation to China: the revolt of Huan Ch'ao in 878. This rebellion led to the massacre of the colony of Muslim merchants in Guangzhou and started a complex period that would eventually bring down the Tang dynasty (Hourani 1979 [1951]: 76-9; al-Mas'ūdī 1861-7, I: 307-8). The involution of the 'advances' achieved in the early Islamic period is considered a result of the failure of the state to maintain its authority and the whole model.

The Islamicate model of Islamization in the Gulf, therefore, has the growth of the Islamic state at its core. In this model, the area was brought under Islam quite early and the Gulf Arabs became steadfast supporters of the Caliphate. Cities then started to emerge under the protection of the Abbasid state and trade was boosted by the demand that they generated, leading to higher levels of connectivity, development and demographic growth. When the state structures failed to offer that protection, the whole system collapsed.

Problems with the Islamicate model

As with the case of al-Andalus, the evidence of the processes of state creation and consolidation, urban development and expansion of connectivity is quite solid; however, the thread bringing them together to shape the narrative of Islamization according to the Islamicate model can be put into question. Several problems emerge when looking with some attention at the whole timeline of the phenomena discussed above.

The first issue to note has to do with the almost causal relationship established between the creation of the Islamic polity, the foundation of trade cities and the peak of connectivity (represented by the establishment of direct routes to China). However, the timeline of events suggests instead that the increase of connectivity can be dated to the period immediately after the Islamic expansion in the Gulf, and some time *before* the network of cities had been created. After the creation of Basra as a *miṣr* in Iraq (637), there are no documented foundations of cities in the Gulf until Sohar (*c.* 650–700), Baghdad (762), Siraf (*c.* 750–800) and, if we are ready to consider it as a sort of town, Murwab (*c.* 800). However, we know of the existence of merchant colonies with the mention of 'Persians' and 'Muslims' in Hainan (South China Sea) in 748, in Yangzhou (East China) in 760 and possibly in Guangzhou (South China) in 758 (for sure in 878) (see Carvajal López 2017 for a review of sources of these dates). This means that the flow of merchants from the Middle East to China predated the foundation of Baghdad and several cities of the Gulf. Therefore, it is difficult to argue that cities were the engines behind the expansion in connectivity, and it seems more likely that they emerged out of it and perhaps pushed it further.

The role of sedentarization in the Islamicate model needs to be re-evaluated as well. As we have seen above, the model suggests that the same state that was founding cities eventually absorbed nomads and forced or seduced them into sedentarization. However, the processes of sedentarization of nomads, at least in its earlier stages, do not seem to be tied to the process of urban expansion. The site of Murwab, presented above, is quite exceptional, both in terms of its size and of its link with a fort. Most of the establishments of permanent or semi-permanent settlements by nomads that can be documented in the Gulf tend to take the form of small villages with the shape and size of nomadic campsites and without any clear relationship with fortifications. In Qatar there are several examples (see villages described in Carter and Stremke 2021; Carvajal López, Roberts et al 2018; 2020; Macumber 2016; McPhillips et al 2015). Outside Qatar, a similar site has been documented in Kuwait (Kennet et al 2013). The dating of these archaeological sites is key. They have been generally dated to the ninth century for the resemblance of their material culture to that of Murwab (e.g. Macumber 2016; McPhillips et al 2015). However, radiocarbon dates of the excavation of one small site, Yughbī, placed it firmly in the seventh to eighth century, with only squatters' reoccupation in the ninth century (Carvajal López, Roberts et al 2020). This means that the foundation of Yughbī happened not only before that of Murwab, but also before that of Baghdad and the main cities of the Gulf (Sohar and Siraf), with the only exception of Basra (which has a very different history). Similar dates (seventh to ninth centuries) have been proposed recently for the other sites of Qatar too (Carter and Stremke 2021). Therefore, it would be reasonable to suggest that the phenomenon of the permanent or semipermanent villages predates that of cities.

Although sedentarizing nomads predated cities, it is clear that they were engaged in long distance and regional trade. In fact, their visibility in the archaeological record depends on it, as their campsites can be dated thanks to imported materials. In some cases, the richness of the material culture that they enjoyed, and the range of provenances are quite shocking. In Yughbī, for example, ceramics from as far as Iraq, South Iran and India were documented, as well as significant amounts of glass, metal and stone objects from a variety of sites that could encompass Iran and other places in Arabia (more details on this below). Similar cases can be made for other sites of Qatar and for Kadhima in Kuwait.

These small, non-urban sites were not the only ones, apart from cities, that were engaged in the connectivity of the Gulf. There is evidence of other sedentary places where links to long-distance and regional trade are documented around the eighth century as well. Some of them have been identified as monastic establishments (Bonnéric 2020; 2021; Carter 2013; Carter and Naranjo Santana 2011; Gachet-Bizollon 2011; Insoll et al 2021; Lic 2017). Others seem to have been villages in the interior (Insoll 2005; Sasaki and Sasaki 2011) or nearby the coast (Makharadze et al 2017: 181–2; Di Miceli 2021; Sasaki 1996; Sasaki and Sasaki 1996; 1998; 2000). The panorama that emerges is one where small places belonging to sedentarizing nomads or to settled groups are connected to very distant places since well before the foundation of some of the most important cities in the Gulf.

But this variety is not unique to the period before the emergence of the cities in the Gulf. These constellations of small places, nomadic, semi-nomadic and sedentary seem to have existed during the whole Islamization period in the Gulf, in parallel with the network of cities.

Only this can explain the different patterns of interconnection and connection to distant places of the areas of the Gulf that are observed in the works of Derek Kennet (2012) and Seth Priestman (2021). Kennet has noted how the diverse parts of the Gulf (Iraq, South Iran, Eastern Arabia, the Musandam Peninsula – with its Emirati and its Omani territories – and the rest of Oman) show different degrees of engagement with the networks of the Gulf between the fifth and the fifteenth centuries, as evidenced by the visibility of their settlement patterns in each period. Priestman has analyzed, in detail, ceramic data from six well-known sites of the Gulf between the sixth and the thirteenth century: Busherh and Siraf in South Iran, Kush and Ṣīr Banī Yās (UAE), Bilād al-Qadīm (Bahrein) and Sohar (Oman), showing a range of patterns of consumption and distribution quite diverse and variable.

In absolute numbers it is correct to say that interconnectivity grew in general and that the urban network became more solid and diversified. However, it would be a mistake to reduce the whole galaxy of interconnections of the Gulf in the early Islamic period to the ones developed by urban and sedentary groups protected by the state. Archaeologists' research clearly shows that early Islamic-period interconnectivity is a phenomenon where agents other than the state and towns were involved. It is therefore possible to think that there were other ways to conceive the Islamic as well, ways that would be more significant to the smaller, non-urban communities: nomads and sedentary, Muslims, Christians or otherwise.

An Islamic assemblage in Yughbī (Qatar)

My contribution to the research on Islamic communities in the early Islamic period in the Gulf is focused on the archaeological site of Yughbī, first recorded by Beatrice de Cardi (1978) and re-analyzed in the framework of the Crowded Desert Project.[9] Yughbī was a sedentary or semisedentary site created by a previously nomadic group that built permanent houses at some point between the late-seventh and late-eighth century (Umayyad period). Its size was small: it was composed of a total of perhaps ten buildings, five of which have been investigated with some detail. The phases of the site are well-contextualized and dated with AMS radiocarbon dates. They include Phase I (dated between 532 and 670),[10] when Yughbī was a campsite where nomads returned recurrently; Phase II (674–778 at 2 sigma),[11] when permanent buildings were erected and then abandoned; and Phase III (760–882 at 2 sigma),[12] defined by a possibly sporadic reoccupation of some structures. The almost absolute majority of the material culture recovered at Yughbī belongs to Phase II. It features a relatively large number of objects (for a recently settled nomadic community), most of them ceramics, but also metal, glass, shell and stone. More than the quantity, however, it is the range of provenances of the artefacts that calls for an explanation. The single most abundant category of ceramics is the turquoise-glazed products, containers and tablewares made probably in Iraq, perhaps in Basra. Other categories of ceramics identified have been traced back to Iraq, Iran and, very significantly, some utility and cooking wares are clearly from India (based on provenances established in Kennet 2004 and Priestman 2021). The metal and glass objects are probably manufactured in Iran, and there are steatite vessels that have been most likely produced in Oman or in the Hijaz (see Carvajal López, Roberts et al 2020 for arguments on provenance of these objects). It is very clear that, despite its small size, Yughbī was very well connected to the networks of eighth-century Gulf.

The intense links of Yughbī with the rest of the Gulf should not be considered, however, as anything particularly exceptional, as it has been noted above. Its location in the interior, but not far away from the sea, made it possible for its inhabitants to practise a range of economic activities that could have included pastoralism, fishing, pearl-fishing, trade and military services. This, in fact, could have been the reason why Yughbī was chosen as a place to establish permanent dwellings: it was next to a source of water (a *rawḍa*, or silty depression, with a well in the desert) and it was close to different economic niches. This is again seen in every other similar site in Qatar (cf. Carter and Stremke 2021). Nothing suggests that Yughbī is not an average site.

One unresolved aspect of Yughbī, however, is the faith of the community that inhabited it. No piece of material culture found is indicative of the religious adscriptions of its dwellers. The site of Murwab, about 3 km away and dated only about a century later, had the remains of two mosques (Guérin and Al-Naʿīmī 2009), but no mosque could be identified among the buildings of Yughbī. Assuming they were Muslims, it is perfectly possible that the recently settled nomads of the community continued using yet unfound temporary structures for praying, or even that they did not have them in the settlement. They might have been using a praying space outside the settlement in common with other groups, or they simply may be very early practitioners and the use of the mosques was not solidly established in rural areas yet.[13] It is also possible that the inhabitants of Yughbī were Christians; as noted above, Christianity was thriving in the early Islamic period (and Carter and Stremke highlight the similarities of some of the plans of the sites of Qatar with monasteries). A mixed alternative is also possible. Fred McGraw Donner has suggested the existence of a significant difference between the meaning of 'believer' (*mu'min*, from *amānu*, 'to have faith') and *muslim* (from *aslāmu*, 'to surrender') during the first century of the history of Islam (2010) (cf. Chapter 1). According to Donner, the Believers would form a core group within the Islamic community, distinguished by their sincerer and stricter adherence to Islamic doctrine. The Muslims, instead, were less zealous, but were political allies who accepted the authority of the Prophet and of the Caliphs afterwards. In this sense, this first meaning of Muslim was not necessarily exclusive of other religious adherences, and made it possible for Pagans, Jewish and Christians to be members of the Islamic community as long as they were subordinated to the Islamic leader. The inhabitants of Yughbī could very well have fallen within this category of early Muslims.

However, I believe that the lack of clear evidence of the religious adscription of the inhabitants of Yughbī can be considered a blessing in disguise, since it invites us to consider aspects of their beliefs from a wider perspective, less concerned with labels that had very different meanings in the seventh and eighth centuries, and more inclusive of the conditions in which their lives and their worldviews developed. This amounts to a consideration of the different assemblages enfolded together.

In my search for these assemblages, I will point out what I consider to be the most interesting among the elements retrieved in the excavation of Yughbī. It is a set of twenty-five net weights uncovered in a primary position. They had all been threaded together in a string that had hung off a wall on one of the buildings in Yughbī; when the wall collapsed, the set of weights were conserved below the rubble until they were unearthed by archaeologists in 2018. The careful documentation of the set allowed for the reconstruction of the position in which they would have been together. The weights probably belonged to a cast net that could have been using for fishing or for catching birds, or they could have been simply used as spare parts for replacements to fix nets (cf. Donaldson 1979: 120–32; Jansen van Rensburg 2016: 127–33; 137–8). Weights like these are very often documented in archaeological excavations of the Gulf (see Carvajal López, Roberts et al 2020: 68 for a full list of references), but a set like this, well threaded together, is not as frequent, and allows for a better understanding of the community of beings (including humans and non-humans) in Yughbī (Figure 5.4, Table 5.2).

The manufacture of the weights of the set shows a deeper trajectory of each one of them, encompassing several assemblages at the same time. All the weights were ceramic, with the exception of one, carved out of a stone. Among the ceramic ones, four of them were shaped directly from clay (as the burr around their holes indicate), but the rest were carved out of sherds of larger, discarded ceramic vessels, identifiable up to a certain extent. Five of these belonged to Torpedo jars, a type of large amphora covered with bitumen on the inside to make them waterproof. The suggested provenance of the Torpedo jars is Southern Iraq (TORP: Priestman 2021, II: 41–5). Two other weights were made of sherds of imported vessels: one of turquoise-glazed jars, made in Iraq (TURQ: Kennet 2004: 36–7; Priestman 2021, II: 89–91)

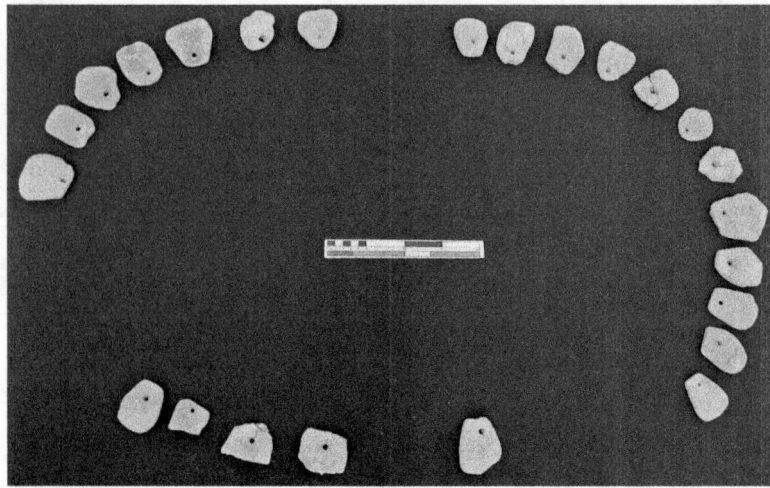

Figure 5.4 A set of net weights found in Yughbī and abandoned in Phase I (*c.* 674–778 CE). The disposition of the items is as ascertained from their *in situ* position. Picture from the Crowded Desert Project.

and one from a ceramic fabric identified as hard lime-spalled ware (HARLIM: *ibidem*: 19–21). Finally, thirteen weights were made from ceramic vessels very common in Yughbī, but probably not made in Qatar (as there is no known ceramic source there); the provenance of these vessels could be from Southern Iran, as the Sirafi wares are the closest parallels in terms of shapes and fabrics, but provenance analysis needs to be undertaken.

It is safe to say that the set of weights represents a variety of objects and types coming from a range of places, and therefore it reflects the connectivity of Yughbī in the Gulf. This is a 'hard' assemblage of elements engaged among themselves that is not only indicative of the reach of connections, but also of their intensity. Indeed, the availability of sherds of the density and size appropriate to be reworked as weights must have been possible because the vessels themselves were imported, used, discarded and broken with sufficient frequency. Finally, the relationships of interconnectivity mapped by this assemblage can easily be extended as lines of flight connecting other elements of the site:

Table 5.2 Data about the net weights retrieved in Phase II of Yughbi. Key: Wgt = Weight in g; Th = Average thickness in cm; Wdt = Maximum width in cm; Lgt = Maximum length in cm. Data from the Crowded Desert Project

Find no	Shape	Material	Macroscopic fabric	Wgt	Th	Wdt	Lgt	Comments
23	Trapezoid	Pottery	Common	69	1.3	6.7	6.8	White slip outside
34	Short trapezoid	Pottery	Common	33	0.9	4.6	6.3	Half surface exterior gone, white slip
18	Rough pentagon	Pottery	Common	73	1.1	7.5	8.4	White slip outside
35	Square	Pottery	Common	44	1	5.3	6	White slip outside
17	Rough pentagonal trapezoid	Pottery	Common	45	1	5.9	7	White slip outside
25	Trapezoid	Pottery	Common	58	1.6	6	6.9	Remains of white slip outside
19	Trapezoid	Pottery	Common	57	1.2	6	7.2	White slip outside
26	Elongated square	Pottery	Common	43	0.9	5.2	7.2	Burnt marks outside
27	Trapezoid	Pottery	Common	58	1.2	6.5	7.1	Burnt marks outside
13	Rough pentagon	Pottery	Common	68	1.3	5.2	8.1	
31	Trapezoid	Pottery	Common	43	0.7	6.3	7.2	Broken in one corner
20	Inverted fusiform	Pottery	Common	46	0.9	5.5	7.2	
14	Inverted fusiform	Pottery	TORP	31	0.9	5.5	6.7	Weathered, darkened in both surfaces
16	Inverted fusiform	Pottery	TORP	27	1.2	5.1	5.6	Weathered, darkened in internal surface
29	Trapezoid	Pottery	TORP	61	1.7	5.7	6.2	Weathered, darkened in internal surface, remains of white slip outside
15	Square	Pottery	Common	51	1.3	5.5	6.5	
32	Inverted fusiform	Pottery	Specific	57	1.5	5.2	6.3	Standardized, specifically made, burr around hole
11	Inverted fusiform	Pottery	Specific	56	1.8	4.9	6.2	Standardized, specifically made, burr around hole

(*Continued.*)

Table 5.2 Continued.

Find no	Shape	Material	Macroscopic fabric	Wgt	Th	Wdt	Lgt	Comments
22	Inverted fusiform	Pottery	Specific	52	1.3	5	6.3	Standardized, specifically made, burr around hole and inside it
21	Rounded and cut	Pottery	TORP	54	1.4	5.2	7.4	Remains of bitumen inside
33	Square (broken)	Pottery	LISV?	22	0.8	4	4.4	
12	Elongate square	Pottery	TURQ	67	1.6	5.1	7.1	Remains of green glaze in both sides
24	Elongate square	Pottery	TORP	47	1.2	4.7	6.7	
30	Trapezoid	Pottery	Specific	67	1.1	5.5	7.3	Specifically made, burr around hole and inside it, probably fusiform originally, now with a lost corner.
28	Irregular	Stone	81	1.5	5.2	6.3	28	Irregular

other ceramic types, metal and glass artefacts, organic material-like shells, specific know-how materialized in the buildings and people themselves (who could be coming from and going to different parts of the Gulf). These assemblages indicate that Yughbī was indeed a community of beings that extended well beyond the limits of the site that was excavated.

Moreover, it can be said that Yughbī was a community of Islamic beings, whether its inhabitants were Muslims or not. These beings were part of the critical events for Islamic history that were happening at the same time that the buildings in Yughbī were erected, in the seventh and eighth centuries: the expansion of Islam over Eastern Arabia first and over Iran afterwards, the anti-caliphate of Qaṭarī ibn al-Fujāʻa, the sedentarization of nomads and the rise of urban communities associated with long-distance trade in the Gulf. The people in Yughbī were involved in all this as pastoralists, peasants, fishermen, craftspeople, warriors, traders or simply as consumers of goods and stories. They were shaped by relationships with things, animals and plants coming from different part of the Gulf that were, in turn, being shaped by those relationships too. Whether the inhabitants of Yughbī were Muslims or not is a moot question when faced with this panorama; it would be difficult to get a clearer vision of the relationships that gave rise to Islamic Con-Text and to Islamic beings.

Some conclusions

The two case studies presented above have the criticism of the Islamicate model of Islamization in common. In this model, Islamization is presented as the result of the expansion of the Islamic polity and the adoption of a relatively strong state, the centrality of the urban world, a cosmopolitan way of life and a strong connectivity that kept trade networks alive to support the consumption and taxes that made all the parts of the model sustainable. The criticism of the Islamicate model does not reject the existence or even the centrality of these elements, but questions the connection made between all of them (threaded differently in each area of study) and, above all, their need for the creation of Islamic Con-Text. In other words, these are not the only conditions under which Islamization is possible, and they are not even the only or the best conditions for Islamization of the early Islamic period. In order to have as complete an understanding of Islamization as possible, we need to reject the idea that there are more or less correct or purer ways of Islamization.

Islamization, that is, the creation of Islamic Con-Text, is underpinned by phenomena of creation of meaning. From the perspective of Islamic beings, the expansion of Con-Text is not a purely intellectual endeavour happening in a vacuum, but the alignment of material conditions of life with the expectations and structures inherited from previous Con-Textual situations. From a perspective configured by assemblage theory, Islamization is the alignment of the different assemblages at a particular scale that generates Islamic meanings and beings. Scale here can be understood in its historical and geographical meaning, but it can also encompass other dimensions.

The Vega of Granada is a relatively small geographical area, but the depth of its history, the amount of information that we have from the early Islamic period and the volume of research accumulated over more than a century of studies means that there are multiple scales on which assemblages can be accommodated. Mapping the assemblage of cooking pots on the one side and of the large containers on the other, it is possible to trace the lines of flight of stratified assemblages, revealing an accumulation of processes of technology dispersion and coalescence, social groups and political institutions between the eighth and the tenth centuries. By the end of the tenth century, however, the dispersion of technology seems to attenuate, and coalescence predominates, suggesting that a more homogeneous, harmonic Islamization (generation of Islamic Con-Text) has been reached. A caveat is needed here: harmonic Islamization is not the same as social harmony. In fact, the eleventh century is, in terms of *événementielle* history, one of the more eventful periods in the Vega of Granada,[14] starting with the sack of Ilbīra in 1011, following with the bellicose Zirid state and culminating with the

Almoravid invasion in 1090. However, during this remarkable century there seems to be a more stable agreement on how to differentiate (frame) and differenciate (actualize) Islamic beings, and so at this scale, Islamic Con-Text seems firmly territorialized.

In contrast to the case study of the Vega of Granada, the early Islamic-period Gulf needs to be framed on a simpler scale, despite being a much larger geographical area and having a deeper history. I believe that the lack of research and information plays a very relevant role here. Most of what is known of the Gulf comes from extrapolation of different areas, or, in other words, from extending the lines of flight of assemblages. This is not necessarily wrong but makes it clear that there is much work to do to adjust the scales of Islamic Con-Text in the Gulf. A simple assemblage in this area, a set of net weights found in the Islamic site of Yughbī, has been taken as reference of Islamization. The mapping of this assemblage and its stratification with others in the archaeological site and in the wider archaeological context, shows a much more homogeneous and linear Islamization than that of the Vega of Granada, at least at the scale that we can use to analyze processes. There are no contradictory moves of dispersion and coalescence. On the contrary, the analysis shows that the creation of Islamic Con-Text was underpinned by a steady deterritorialization of the nomadic way of life and the territorialization of a sedentary and much widely connected way of life that matches wider political and historical processes. Although sedentarism seems to deterritorialize again later (around the tenth century), the connected way of life of the Islamic beings of the Gulf was there to last even through the periods where the power of the state and the urban world seemed to be waning.

In conclusion, the combination of the theories of Ahmad and Deleuze in understanding Islamization in archaeology provides interesting insights on the historical processes. The generation of Islamic Con-Text (that is, Islamization) has to be understood over a particular scale within which it is possible to find clues to understand the process in which Islamic beings can be conceived virtually (differentiated) and actualized (differenciated).

6

Conclusion

This final chapter offers an overview of the different ideas about Islam and Islamization presented in this work, with the aim of providing a more systematic proposal in consonance with the theoretical approach presented throughout this book. A brief summary of the chapters of the book is necessary.

Chapter 1 offers an introduction to the concept of Islam, departing from the definition provided in the *Encyclopaedia of Islam*. It became clear that, from a cultural point of view, it was not possible to disentangle the concept from a tension between faith and action. This tension has dominated cultural studies on Islam (including those of anthropologists and archaeologists). The problem of this tension consists in that it is framed in a conception of religion that emerges in the history of Western thought and that tends to establish a neat separation between religiosity and any other aspects of culture. Therefore, social phenomena related to the Islamic are considered as a separate sphere of cultural life, making them commensurable with phenomena related to Christianity and other religions. A second related problem is the connection of this religious sphere with that of cultural life: given the evidently strong bond between the two spheres in the Islamic world, Western thought has often considered that there is a relationship of power between the two, which is manifested in the orthodoxy of practices and forms. The closer to the orthodoxy that the manifestations of Islam are, the purer they are; the less orthodox, the more contaminated with influences of other ideas. These two problems have been highlighted and challenged by the definition of the Islamic by Shahad Ahmed (2016), who considers that at the core of Islam there is not so much orthodoxy as hermeneutical engagement. This engagement, undertaken by Islamic people, is an exploration of the world that is given (Text or Pre-Text) in search of the Truth and Meaning of the Revelation (Con-Text). There are no purer or more contaminated versions of Islam: there is simply a wide field of meanings (Con-Text, again) with space for variety, disagreement and even contradiction. This field is characterized not by convergence of opinions, but by mutual intelligibility: all partakers can understand the discourse and feelings of the other, whether they agree or not. Moreover, Con-Text is eminently historical: it is different across time and place, and even across scales (we will come back to that later). But the history of Islamic Con-Text is not the same as the history of Islam: it is the history *that Islam makes* at any given time. What this chapter introduced, therefore, is the need to consider the history of Islam and Islamization *in their own terms*.

In Chapter 2, I charted the main approaches to Islamization by archaeologists and historians working in different historical scenarios. Some conceptions of Islamization equate it with conversion to Islam, thus overlooking an explanation of the cultural aspects of the process (and assuming problematic positions on the relationship between religion and culture). More nuanced views tend to downplay the role of religion and focus more on cultural change. The works of Richard Bulliet on conversion in the early Islamic period (1979) and of Manuel Acién on the formation of al-Andalus (1997 [1994]) are different, but they are both dependent on a model of Islamization based not so much on conversion, but on the transformation of social relationships, to the extent that religion becomes almost ancillary. Both models are very close to the tension between Islamic and Islamicate created by Marshall Hodgson (1974), which Ahmed has criticized in line with the problems denounced above. More recent models of Islamization, and more effective ones, are those where conversion and cultural change are brought together in a phased transformation, as done by Richard Eaton in East Bengal (1993) and by Tim Insoll in Sub-Saharan Africa (2003) and Ethiopia (2017). However, the problem with these approaches is that, in searching to offer a measure of how Islamized societies are in different phases, they maintain a separation between Islam and society that is difficult to conciliate with Ahmed's perspective.

The separation between Islam and society is also a problem when trying to reconcile Islamic identity and dualist conceptions of the world. In Chapter 3 I have analyzed the work of Gabrielle Marranci (2008), a most detailed attempt to thread together a study of Muslims with a concept of identity based on neuroscientific conceptions of mind and body. Marranci's attempt to explain Islamic identity from the point of view of feelings and identity is ultimately unsuccessful because he places Islam firmly outside the mind and therefore in a place beyond the reach of his own theoretical approach. For him, Islam is a 'map of discourses', but he ultimately does not explain what is specific in it to produce Islamic identity. In this chapter it becomes apparent that Islam needs to be constitutive of Islamic beings, because it cannot be exclusively outside or inside them. Incidentally, this is one consequence of Ahmed's theory too. Islamic beings develop Islamic Con-Text, but they are also shaped by it, in a way that it is not possible to conceive them without Islam.

In Chapter 4, I have reached the theoretical core of this book by bringing together what I consider to be the most salient aspects of Ahmed's ideas for archaeologists – those related to Con-Text – and new materialist and posthumanist theory based mainly on the works of Gilles Deleuze and Félix Guattari (1983 [1977]; 1987 [1980]). The archaeological application of these ideas is based on a wide range of works, but I have been most influenced by archaeologists Ben Jervis (2018), Rachel Crellin (2020) and Oliver Harris (2021). In this chapter I extend the idea of Islamic beings of Ahmed to non-humans and transform the Con-Text of Islamic Truth and Meaning in an assemblage that is linked with other assemblages by vertical and horizontal relationships. Vertical relationships are constituted in the process of the enfolding of different assemblages by structures of codification and territorialization. Horizontal relationships emerge in the limits of the assemblages, defined by the mapping of their lines of flight and by the extent of their relationships of interiority and exteriority. This allows us to understand Islamization through the mapping of the Islamic Con-Textual assemblage, of its vertical and horizontal relationships. Scale becomes a key issue: Islamization cannot be defined as a process with a clear beginning and an end outside of a scale. It is about change in Con-Text, which can only be grasped by mapping changes in its own assemblage and the ones enfolding it.

I have offered two examples of what this approach should look like in Chapter 5, where I have analyzed the Islamization of the Vega of Granada (Spain) and of Qatar (in the Arabian-Persian Gulf) during the early Islamic period. In both cases, I have explained the assumptions about Islamization that exist in current scholarship and how they are tinted by a model of Islamicate society *á la* Hodgson. This does not necessarily mean the models are wrong, but they are partial and do not cover the whole spectra of the Islamization phenomena. I have offered an alternative, more nuanced perspective by focusing on the Islamization of small assemblages of objects as a way to understand the general conditions of each context (and Con-Text).

In this final chapter I wish to return to the theoretical plane of my work and review some of the different views on Islamization that have emerged in the text with the aim of bringing them together in a coherent and useful conclusion.

What is Islamization?

Traditionally Islamization has been presented as the process of transformation of a non-Islamic society into an Islamic one.[1] From this perspective, the process of analysis of Islamization consists of finding 'markers' of how Islam is gaining hold in the identities, beliefs and practices of people. However, there is a problem associated to this perspective: it misrepresents Islam from a purely Islamic or Con-Textual point of view. It could be said that it is an answer to a wrong question.

From an Islamic point of view, the whole universe is a manifestation of God and therefore it has always been 'Islamic'. What changes with the arrival of the Prophet and the Revelation is that God's Message becomes accessible to everyone by means of accepting it, that is, submission (*islām*). That is why the pre-Islamic period is generally called *Jāhiliyya*, that is, 'Ignorance' in Arabic.[2] But Ahmed makes it clear that historically it has been possible to submit to God's Message and to Islam by searching for the Revelation in other ways than the acceptance of the literal content of the Quran and the Hadith (Text), that is, in Pre-Textual ways, such as art (Ahmed 2016: 408–25), science (*ibidem*: 430–5), music (425–30), rulership (*ibidem*: 453–82) or even violence (*ibidem*: 452). In other words, Islam does not consist of the mere acceptance of a more or less orthodox content of core ideas and practices: it is a whole different way of being in the world, that is, of establishing relationships between the self, other human and non-human beings, and God. This is what we can call, following Ahmed, Con-Text.

The centrality of Con-Text presents a problem to the understanding of Islamization as the expansion of Islam, because from an internal perspective, everything within Con-Text is Islamic somehow. Even the past. It is not possible to conceive something as non-Islamic from within, and this is why the pre-Islamic past cannot be considered non-Islamic: it is simply not-quite-Islamic-yet. But within Con-Text it is possible to perceive different forms and intensities of the Islamic; within each form, there is an amount of virtuality (not-yet-fully-Islamic) and actuality (Islamic-at-last). The transition between virtual and actual forms is what makes Islamization possible and is what keeps the momentum of the becoming of the Islamic Con-Textual assemblage.

The centrality of Con-Text in Islamization does not present any problem to consider non-Muslims and non-human beings within the Islamic assemblage. Ahmed is clear in stating that non-Muslims can also engage with Con-Text, because what makes Con-Text is meaning, not faith or action. Even non-Muslim people can make actions meaningful, that is, intelligible, within a Con-Textual framework if they are embedded in it. By the same token, non-human beings are within Con-Text when they are constituted in part with Islamic meaning. As it has been noted in Chapter 4, Islamic meaning is acquired through relationships. It is for this reason that Deleuzean metaphysics are appropriate to deal with the question of what Islamic is: it is not a matter of identifying oneself with Islam (something that, in dualist metaphysics, only people can do); it is a matter of being Islamic in virtuality and/or in actuality.

The discussion above shows why the question of the transition from a non-Islamic society to an Islamic society is problematic. It is simply the wrong question from an Islamic perspective because it assumes that a non-Islamic state of being is possible. By posing the question in this sense, we place ourselves outside a Con-Textual assemblage and enter a different one. In my case, and in the case of most academic scholars, we usually contemplate the problem from a Western humanist and dualist mindset. Islamization here becomes a different thing: a change that cannot be quite grasped and needs to be approached by making Islam as analogous as possible to something that is commensurable within a Western mindset: a belief, a practice, an ideology, an orthodoxy, a discourse, etc. This becomes particularly more complicated to grasp in modern Islam, where the separation of religion and culture has been assumed by Muslims themselves (Ahmed 2016: 185–9). This does not make Muslims non-Islamic, out of Con-Text. As in the case of non-Muslims living in Con-Textual scenarios, Muslims can place themselves outside Con-Text and adopt non-Con-Textual meaning in their daily lives. Following Deleuzean metaphysics, this is not a mere change of perspective: it is an ontological change, as Muslims and non-Muslims are now beings emerging from assemblages different to Islamic Con-Text. I will follow this thought further below.

Let us return to Islamic Con-Text. Here, Islamization can be defined as the movement towards differenciation or actualization of the Islamic forms that exist as virtual. This means that, on the one hand, Islamization is a process that is continuously happening in any Islamic community. It does not start in a pre-Islamic society and end in a 'fully' Islamic one. It goes from a state of being Islamic to another one where Islam is manifested more intensely. On the other hand, it means that Islamization is connected in a vertical dimension with the actualization of other assemblages that are enfolded with that of Con-Text. The study of phenomena of transformation in a range of different scales, from landscapes to ceramic vessels, can offer clues on the changes operating in Islamic Con-Text. It must be emphasized that Islamic Con-Text does not follow other assemblages any more than the latter follows the former: there are no links of cause and effect. The assemblages are enfolded together and influence each other in vertical relationships.

However, understanding Islamization only as a general process is not the aim of an archaeologist (or a historian). A historical consideration of Islamization requires, in fact, delimiting scales. Once a scale is determined, tipping points, gradients, phases and even the definition itself of Islamic beings, emerges from the Islamic Con-Text. The comparison of different scales is possible by focusing on different enfolded assemblages and it offers the most nuanced view of Islamization that we can achieve. Therefore, the selection of a particular scale to explore will determine the set of assemblages more appropriate for our study. The knowledge of lines of flight, territorialization and coding of those assemblages will help us to map the Islamic Con-Textual assemblage, and thus Islamization.

It is possible to map Islamization without actually understanding it. This is because it is possible to map the assemblages enfolded with Con-Text without ever reaching its true shape. I argue that the only way to do this is to *become Islamic* in the sense defended in this book.

Becoming Islamic (but not necessarily Muslim)

I have established above that Islamization, in its Con-Textual sense, can only be understood within Con-Text. A pertinent question, therefore, would be: 'How to access Con-Text?' The theoretical basis of this book, the works of Ahmed and Deleuze, offer different solutions that are not necessarily the same, but are not necessarily opposed either.

Ahmed's *Being Islamic* is based on the analysis of what he calls the Balkans-to-Bengal complex, that is, the cultural mosaic that emerged between the Ottoman, Safavid and Mughal empires between the fourteenth and nineteenth centuries. However, he did not limit his concepts to that historical scenario: the hermeneutical engagement with Text, Pre-Text and Con-Text is a feature that defines Islam all over history, and in all communities that practise it, within Islamic societies or not. I will go beyond that to suggest that, following the large expansion of Islam in the early stages of its history, we could consider that, *to some extent, human history has become Islamic.*

This is a very different perspective from the one that can be derived from Samuel Huntingdon's narrative of clash of civilizations (1996), where Islam is defined as an alternative way to construct society to that of Western capitalism (and a threat to it as well). This seems to be little more than an updated version of the classic Orientalist perception of Islam (and the East in general) as outside of the progression of human history, represented by the West, which was also adopted by some socialist thinkers (cf. criticism raised by Amin 1974 and Barceló 1978). Although modern scholarship on Islamic studies does not follow these ideas, the definition of what Islam is precisely in terms that can be understood within a Western mindset is still a challenging one if a reductionist approach wants to be avoided (cf. Chapter 1). The historical relevance of Islam in history, and its contributions to (Western) knowledge in particular, are now well-known and generally celebrated (e.g. Iqbal 2012; Vernet 1999), but the main narrative of history still remains too tied to a quintessential Western sense of progression to which everything else is subordinated. To become aware of the general Islamization of history consists in accepting that there is a whole different body of knowledge, a perception of the past and the future that is relevant for millions of human beings, and yet it is mostly unknown or misunderstood within the frame of Western education and scholarship. It also implies the recognition of the need to engage with that body of knowledge outside the boundaries of the Western senses of commensurability and intelligibility in search of mutual understanding, something that at least Islamic archaeologists have been wary of doing in general. Finally, coming to terms with the idea that there are things that we ignore about Islam brings us to the position where we wonder, ask, discuss and learn about Con-Text; because we will be engaging meaningfully with Islam.

There is an answer to this question from the perspective of Deleuzean metaphysics as well. If we adopt assemblage theory, then we must note that our own being is as much the result of an assemblage of elements as something else. Therefore, we become Islamic by engaging with the Islamic Con-Text in as much as we are pursuing to make it meaningful. We become Islamic beings emerging out of Islamic Con-Text in the same way as other Islamic beings. This is, in Deleuzean terms, the hermeneutical engagement with Islam: the acknowledgement of becoming Islamic.

Becoming Islamic to understand Islamization, therefore, does not involve necessarily a change of religious affiliation. It involves the acknowledgement of our own ignorance on many aspects of Islam (even when we may be very knowledgeable of others) and the willingness to overcome it by *submitting* to other ways of making meaning.

It is needless to state that this is not the last word on Islamization from an archaeological perspective. Many questions must be resolved. Ahmed's impressive work has provided a first step on the consideration of hermeneutic engagement in Islamic archaeology. But my work can only grasp the surface of this immense body of knowledge and relationships that is Con-Text, and which will need to be introduced in archaeological theory in the next few years. Deleuze's philosophy has been fundamental for me to reach a way that I consider satisfactory to define the relationship between Islam and beings, and yet the risk of Deleuzean metaphysics becoming a form of *Westernsplaning* is too large. The engagement with Islamic Con-Text is essential in understanding the Islamic phenomena in its own terms, without imposing any pre-determined ideas on it. The question of orthodoxy is worth commenting on: both Ahmed and Deleuze, each in their own way, reject the centrality of authority in the making of meaning. Meaning must emerge from exploration. The task of scholars is to extend that exploration as far as possible within their own human limitations.

Notes

1 Introduction: Islam and Islamization

1 The references to the *Encyclopaedia of Islam* used in this work are from the latest version of the entry of interest, which is in the Second Edition (*EI2*, compiled between 1960 and 2005). The Third Edition, currently under development (*EI3*, started in 2012), has not developed new versions of the entries relevant for this text.

2 Islamization: From Conversion to Cultural Change

1 It would be unfair, however, not to mention the works of scholars such as Ali Baghat (1923) or Manuel Gómez Moreno (1898), who had a genuine interest in Islamic archaeology to shed light on national origins (Baghat) or local questions (Gómez Moreno), and therefore not necessarily imperialist.
2 It is worth noting that different language-speaking traditions of Islamic archaeology follow different trajectories in this period, and that the English-speaking tradition of Islamic archaeology is a relatively late development in comparison with others, such as the French or the Spanish ones (for the French tradition, see the now disappeared journal *Archéologie Islamique*; for the Spanish tradition, some analysis is offered in Carvajal López 2014; 2020b; Díaz-Andreu 1993).
3 This may be an adaptation of the Arab tribal practice of political alignment of genealogical history. This was achieved by emphasizing kin links with political allies and reorienting or ignoring those links in relation to political adversaries, noted in the early Islamic period (Crone 1980) and in more recent periods (Fabietti 2012). The candidates to the caliphal dignity of the Abbasids and of the Fatimids, for example, claimed lineages linked to the Prophet themselves. In eleventh-century al-Andalus, it was popular for elite urban families to claim ancestry from the tribes that participated in the conquest of the peninsula, very often also linked to the Companions

of Muḥammad. This genealogical interest moved Ibn Ḥazm to write his *Jamhara*, a compilation of genealogical histories (Terés 1957).

4 The theological debate between practice and belief in Islam has been mentioned in Chapter 1.

5 It is worth reminding ourselves of Cantwell Smith's discussion about belief explained in Chapter 1. In his conception of belief as applied to Islam, faith was not a matter of acceptance of dogmata, but of acceptance of a cosmic drama on which there is no option.

6 The biological experiment is described by Bulliet: it consists of the analysis of a population of fruit flies locked in a bottle with a limited amount of food. At the start, the flies are few and reproduce to a lower rate, but as soon as they reach a critical number, their reproduction rates increase very rapidly. When the food supply becomes scarce, the population drops, and so does the reproduction rate.

7 Just to mention some examples of the study of rural areas in countries covered by Bulliet, there is now some extensive literature covering changes in the countryside of the area of Syria and Palestine: see Avni 2014; Magness 2003; Walmsley 2000; 2007. In al-Andalus there is evidence of important changes introduced in the rural communities by tribal groups of Arabs and Berbers immigrated after the Islamic conquest (see the debate mentioned in the following pages, in Chapter 5 and in Barceló et al 1996; Kirchner 2009). For the Persian Gulf, see the works mentioned in Chapter 5 and in particular Kennet 2012.

8 The core readings are the two editions of his book *Entre el Feudalismo y el Islam* (Acién 1997 [1994]) and his article 'La formación social islámica' (Acién 1998), but these two articles are based on the archaeological and historical work that he published before (Acién 1986; 1992). I have already explained Acién's theory and what I considered to be its highlights and its shortcomings in Carvajal López 2014; 2022; forthcoming.

9 Guichard's theory was revolutionary in its time for al-Andalus, because it established, with solid evidence, this rupture that ran counter to what most Spanish scholars had thought for centuries, namely that the Islamic invasion never altered the Catholic essence of the Spanish people (e.g. Sánchez Albornoz 1956). See García Sanjuán 2012 for a review of this historiographical opinion.

10 For more recent appraisals of this discussion, see Boone 2009; Carvajal López 2014; 2019; Glick 1995.

11 As Insoll has noted (2016: 246), a similar model was developed by Trimingham (1968), with his three stages named germination, crisis and reorientation.

3 Islamic Identity and *Being Islamic*

1 A definition that Marranci takes from Gregory Bateson (2002, in Marranci 2006: 49–50), and that he also compares to Homi Babha's 'circle of panic' (Babha 1994: 200, in Marranci 2006: 50).
2 The 'terror suspect' was convicted as a terrorist later on (Rawlinson 2018).
3 Two clarifications must be done at this point. The first one is that Ahmed's definition of humanity does not necessarily imply that people who are not Muslims are not human. As Ahmed explains in extension, non-Muslims can also be engaged hermeneutically in Islam in different ways (see below). The second point to clarify is that Ahmed does not believe that this definition of humanity is ontological in the sense of separating humans from one another, since it is based on knowledge (2016: 376). The concept of ontology in itself is complicated, as it acquires different meanings in metaphysics and philosophy than in anthropology and archaeology (cf. Harris 2021: 44–5). Philosophical ontology refers to what exists (the concept that Ahmed is espousing here), whereas in anthropology and archaeology it may refer to claims about the reality or about radical difference. In some of those senses of the word 'ontology', one could argue that Ahmed *is making an ontological claim about humanity*. This has some important implications that will be discussed in Chapter 4.
4 Arguably in his brief discussion of Islamic art (Ahmed 2016: 408–25) and in the context of criticism to the use of prescriptive Islamic interpretations in the support of the construction of nation states (focusing on the example of the Wahhabism of Saudi Arabia) (*ibidem*: 532–7).
5 The consideration of phases or stages in Islamization can be useful, however, when considering Islamization at different scales, as will be explained in Chapters 4 and 5.
6 These maps are conserved in the *Archivio di Stato di Venezia* and were recovered by Siriol Davies for the Butrint Foundation. They are published now in Davies 2013 and Carvajal López and Palanco Noguerol 2013.

7 The Çams are an Albanian ethnic minority, predominantly Muslim, defined mainly by their southern Tosk dialect (*Arvanitika* in Greece) and by their origin in the region known as Çameria (Threspotia in Greece), which encompasses mainly Southern Epiros (Greece). They were forced to leave Greece in different phases during the first half of the twentieth century, and now live in a diaspora in Albania and other countries, where they consider themselves refugees (Vickers 2002; 2007).

8 For a more complete version of this study on Albania, see Carvajal Lopez 2020a and the report for the Butrint Foundation: Carvajal Lopez et al. 2011.

9 My thanks to Kostas Alexiou, my colleague in the survey, who made possible this fluid communication with the villagers.

4 Islamic Things, Islamic Beings and Con-Text

1 It would be wrong to assume that new materialism exhausts the possibilities of Deleuze's work. It should be merely considered as a particular perspective emerging from his texts, famously written with the intention to be indirect, cryptic and difficult to read. Deleuze refused to use a clear style in order to prevent his work from becoming a closed system of knowledge. Instead, he was searching to excite and inspire new ways of thinking. It is important to note this, because different readings of his work may be used to open different paths in new materialist thinking, or even to challenge it altogether. Flat ontology coming from Latour-based approaches is basically traceable to Deleuze (Fowler 2017: 96), but even within Deleuzian new materialism there are different paths and perspectives (cf. Conneller 2017; Hamilakis 2017 and Lucas 2012; 2017 with the other works listed above). Regarding challenges to new materialism from the Deleuzean field, it has to be stated that not all readers of Deleuze understand his works under the same realist banner than DeLanda and other materialists (Harman 2008: 368). In his reader's guide of *Difference and Repetition*, Joe Hughes considers Deleuze's work as a theory of subjectivity, and though he praises DeLanda's texts in their explanation of Deleuzean non-essentialist metaphysics, he also considers that DeLanda has forced a realist recasting of the philosopher's ontology (Hughes 2009: 183–4).

2   The first Al-Aqṣā Mosque was erected probably during the Umayyad Caliphate of 'Abd al-Mālik (r. 685–705), but the current building is probably based on the building that was built under the rule of the Abbasid Caliph al-Mahdī (r. 744–785) and has seen many subsequent changes (Grafman and Roser-Ayalon 1999). Bowl 21/1965 is a member of the COBALT class as defined by Derek Kennet (2004: 40).
3   This particular bowl would be described as an Islamicate object following Marshall Hodgson's ideas, since it does not seem to have a direct relationship to religion. However, as it is a product of courtly culture of the Abbasid Caliphate, I follow Shahab Ahmed's example and consider it an Islamic object on the basis that it comes from a context (and a Con-Text) marked by the patronage of the caliphs.
4   The denomination of the Mosque-Cathedral of Cordoba responds to a tradition of relatively positive reception of the Islamic past in Spain (despite a long history of rejection: see Carvajal López, Živković et al 2020). A reflection of this dual inheritance can be seen in the recent controversy sparked by the registration of the monument as a property of the Church, considered by many as a usurpation of public property. The administration of the Town Council of Cordoba commissioned an expert report that concluded that the monument was indeed public property and that its registration as a property of the Church had no legal grounds (Carpio Dueñas et al 2018).
5   The metaphor of the map is referred both to assemblages and to strata, which are ultimately the same, as explained below.
6   I have chosen these two particular metaphors of assemblage for my own interest, but the range of definitions and related concepts used by Deleuze and Guattari is immense. A good summary of ideas and concepts can be found in Jervis 2018: Chapter 2.
7   I wish to express my gratitude to Jeffrey Fleisher for kindly providing me with a copy of his paper before publication.
8   I am referring again to the useful adaptation of Deleuzean philosophy to archaeology by Harris 2021: 57. It is also useful to point out briefly the three dimensions that he identifies for the field of intensity: desire, affect and power. These three concepts can be used to define the relational forces that produce difference in an assemblage (*Ibidem*: 58–60).
9   Let us not forget that in Ahmed's theory, non-Muslims can also engage in Con-Text (see Chapter 3 above).

10 This reflection is inspired by similar debates being held between archaeological and anthropological theorists interested in the intersection between new materialism and indigenous ontologies, particularly with First Nations American ones (Cipolla 2020; Crellin 2020: 242–3; Crellin et al 2020: Chapters 5 and 11; Harris 2021: 36–9; Montgomery 2020). To conflate Islamic modes of thought with indigenous ontologies is a mistake, but they both share a subordinate position in the history of European colonialism. Therefore, they are both exposed to the same kind of risk from the perspective of Eurocentric scholarship.

11 For a useful discussion on archaeological time in Deleuzean terms, see Harris 2021: Chapter 7.

12 Of course, scale is still in application here. A scale of analysis encompassing a single molecule allows for a more detailed observation of a tipping point. Large amounts of water suddenly evaporated by a catastrophic event (a volcanic explosion or a meteorite) can produce sudden changes. The concept of phase transition is intimately linked to that of scale.

5 Islamization of Communities: Two Case Studies in Early Islam

1 I owe the term of *Islamicate model* to Eneko López Martínez de Marigorta (2020, in Spanish *modelo islamizado*), who uses it as a way to highlight the coincidences between Marshall Hodgson's and Manuel Acién's ideas. Although this overlap is notable, I think there is some divergence in their approaches that deserves more attention. Hodgson's ideas about culture are reminiscent of Bourdiean distinction and focus on elites, whereas Acién's model looks at society as a whole from a perspective of Marxist ideas about ideological superstructure and infrastructure.

2 My archaeological study of the Vega sets the start of Phase I in *c.* 550 as a way to highlight the continuity of material culture from the pre-Islamic into the Islamic period, but there is no doubt that the innovations described in this chapter are post-711. This has been reflected in Table 5.1 as a separation between Phase Ia (before 711) and Phase Ib (from 711 onwards) (Carvajal López 2022).

3 There is some divergence in dates here, as my intention is to consider only until the end of the Zīrīd state, in 1090. However, in my ceramic analysis I have expanded Phase IV up to the mid-twelfth century, to account for a certain lack of precision in dates of some of the phenomena observed in ceramic production and consumption. That includes the Almoravid period (1090–1147).

4 The data presented in this section are distilled from my previous studies on the ceramics of the Vega of Granada: Carvajal López 2008; 2009; 2012; 2019; Carvajal López and Day 2013; 2015; Carvajal López and Jiménez Puertas 2017; Carvajal López, Hein et al 2018; Jiménez Puertas and Carvajal López 2020; Molera et al 2018; Román Punzón and Carvajal López 2018. The argument presented here has been made in more detail in Carvajal López 2022; forthcoming.

5 In the Middle East they are not identified with the name *alcadafe*, a Spanish substantive suggested by Guillermo Rosselló i Bordoy (1978) to classify this shape. In Palestine, their technical name is simply 'large basins'.

6 Drafts of these contracts have been preserved in juridical sources, as the ones presented in Aguirre Sábada 2000.

7 Hourani (1979 [1951]) convincingly dismissed the possibility of direct navigation of Chinese sailors to the Gulf before the Islamic period, although he believes that Persian sailors could have made it. There were certainly contacts between China and the Middle East before the Islamic period, but the available evidence suggests these were mainly overland or through contacts between different spheres of trade. There is a debate about the early Islamic-period and the direct link between China and the Gulf in literature, which can be followed in these works: in favour: Flecker 2011; George 2015; Schottenhammer 2016; Stargardt 2014; against: Haw 2017. For my own review of all these issues, and my reasoning to support the possibility of direct Islamic navigation between China and the Gulf, see Carvajal López 2017.

8 Avni considers that the sedentarization in the Southern and Western Negev highlands is due to of internal processes of reorganization of the nomadic communities to adapt to new social circumstances. Although his interest in the agency of the nomads is very similar to my own ideas (developed below), Avni also makes them too dependent on the settled people (as it is the former's relationship with the latter that ultimately determines the change of model of subsistence).

9 For information on The Crowded Desert Project, see Carvajal López 2021; Carvajal López et al 2016; Carvajal López et al 2017; Carvajal López, Roberts et al 2018. The excavation of Yughbī is described in detail in Carvajal López, Roberts et al 2020.
10 Dates extracted of samples Beta-504835 (2 Sigma: 532–638 cal AD at 84.8% and 432–489 cal AD at 10.6%), Beta-504840 (2 Sigma: 590–665 cal AD at 95.4%) and Beta-504841 (2 Sigma: 597–670 cal AD at 95.4%).
11 Dates extracted of samples Beta-504836 (2 Sigma: 662–774 cal AD at 95.4%), Beta-504837 (2 Sigma: 664–774 cal AD at 95.4%) and Beta-504838 (2 Sigma: 662–778 cal AD at 92.3%; 842–859 cal AD at 1.6%; 792–804 cal AD at 1.3%; 818–821 cal AD at 0.2%).
12 Dates extracted of sample Beta-504845 (2 Sigma: 760–882 cal-AD at 62.7%; 688–751cal AD at 32.7%). The later chronology is supported by stratigraphy besides this single sample.
13 All conserved mosques that can be dated to the early Islamic period are in urban contexts, with only a few exceptions in farmsteads and in the *quṣūr* of Bilād al-Sham (Avni 1994; 2014). These rural mosques are generally dated between the eighth and the tenth centuries, with the only exception of one recently discovered in Rahal (Israel), dated to the seventh to eighth centuries (Seligman and Ẓur 2021).
14 Also, in al-Andalus, but it is in my interest to keep tied to the geographical scale of the Vega of Granada here.

6 Conclusion

1 And I must confess I myself am guilty of this: Carvajal López 2013. But see Chapter 2 for a more general review.
2 Cf. Peter Webb's (2014) analysis on the meanings of the term Jāhiliyya between the seventh and the thirteenth centuries, showing a range of meanings between a temporal and geographical framework and a 'state of being' (2014: 72). This is in line with the hierarchy of knowledge established by al-Fārābī and mentioned by Ahmed (2016: 376; see also Chapter 3).

Bibliography

Abu Aemar, Ibrahim and Carvajal López, José C. (2014), 'The Pottery of Khirbet Beit Bassa.' *Medieval Ceramics* 35: 1–12.

Acién, Manuel (1986), 'Cerámica a torno lento en Bezmiliana. Cronología, tipos y difusión.' In *I Congreso de Arqueología Medieval Española*, pp. 243–67. Zaragoza: Diputación General de Aragón.

Acién, Manuel (1992), 'Sobre la función de los *ḥuṣūn* en el sur de al-Andalus. La fortificación en el califato.' In *Coloquio Hispano-Italiano de Arqueología Medieval*, pp. 263–74. Granada: Patronato de la Alhambra y el Generalife.

Acién, Manuel [1994] (1997), *Entre el feudalismo y el Islam. 'Umar ibn Ḥafṣūn en los historiadores, en las fuentes y en la historia*. Jaén: Universidad de Jaén.

Acién, Manuel (1998), 'Sobre el papel de la ideología en la caracterización de las formaciones sociales. La formación social islámica.' *Hispania* 200: 915–68.

Agius, Dionisius A. (2008), *Classic Ships of Islam: From Mesopotamia to the Indian Ocean*. Leiden: Brill.

Aguirre Sábada, F. Javier (2000), 'Notas acerca de la proyección de los "kutub al-wata'iq" en el estudio social y económico de al-Andalus.' *Miscelánea de Estudios Árabes y Hebraicos. Sección Árabe-Islam* 49: 3–30.

Ahmed, Shahab (2016), *What is Islam? The Importance of Being Islamic*. Princeton and Oxford: Princeton University Press.

Akbar, Jamel (1989), 'Khaṭṭa and the Territorial Structure of Early Muslim Towns.' *Muqarnas: An Annual of the Visual Cultures of the Islamic World* 6: 22–32.

Alba Calzado, Miguel and Gutiérrez Lloret, Sonia (2008), 'Las producciones de transición al mundo islámico el problema de la cerámica paleoandalusí (siglos VIII y IX).' In Darío Bernal Casasola and Albert Ribera i Lacomba (eds), *Cerámicas Hispanorromanas: Un Estado de la Cuestión*, pp. 585–613. Cádiz: Universidad de Cádiz.

Almagro Gorbea, Antonio (2015), 'Las antigüedades árabes en la Real Academia de San Fernando.' In Antonio Almagro Gorbea (ed.), *El Legado de al-Ándalus: Las Antigüedades Árabes en los Dibujos de la Academia*, pp. 13–29. Granada: Patronato de la Alhambra y el Generalife.

Almagro Gorbea, Antonio and Maier Allende, Jorge (2012), 'Los inicios de la arqueología islámica.' In Antonio Almagro Gorbea and Jorge Maier Allende (eds), *De Pompeya al Nuevo Mundo: La corona española y la arqueología en el siglo XVIII*, pp. 229–44. Madrid: Real Academia de la Historia.

Amorós, Victoria and Gutiérrez Lloret, Sonia (2020), 'Ceramics in Transition: Ceramics from the First Islamic Period in the Western Mediterranean – The Example of Al-Andalus.' *Libyan Studies* 51: 99–125.

Apostolos-Cappadona, Diane (2005), 'Discerning the Hand-of-Fatima. An Iconological Investigation on the Role of Gender in Religious Art.' In Amira El-Azhary Sonbol (ed.), *Beyond the Exotic: Women's Histories in Islamic Societies*, pp. 347–61. New York: Syracuse University Press.

Arthur, Paul (2007), 'Form, Function and Technology in Pottery Production from Late Antiquity to the Early Middle Ages.' In Luke Lavan, Enrico Zanini and Alexander Sarantis (eds), *Technology in Transition AD 300–650*. Late Antique Archaeology vol. 4, pp. 159–86. Leiden: Brill.

Asad, Talal (1986), *The Idea of an Anthropology of Islam*. Washington D.C.: Centre for Contemporary Arab Studies, Georgetown University.

Asad, Talal (1993), *Genealogies of Religion. Discipline and Reasons of Power in Christianity and Islam*. Baltimore and London: The John Hopkins University Press.

Asad, Talal (2009), 'The Idea of an Anthropology of Islam.' *Qui Parle* 17 (2): 1–30.

Avni, Gideon (1996), *Nomads, Farmers and Town-Dwellers: Pastoralist-Sedentist Interaction in the Negev Highlands, Sixth–Eighth Centuries CE*. Jerusalem: Israel Antiquities Authority.

Avni, Gideon (2014), *The Byzantine-Islamic Transition in Palestine: An Archaeological Approach*. Oxford: Oxford University Press.

Bahghat, Ali (1923), 'Les fouilles d'Al Foustat.' *Syria* 4 (1): 59–65.

al-Balādhurī [al-Imām abū-l-'Abbās Aḥmad ibn Jābir al-Balādhurī] (1924), *The Origins of the Islamic State* (vol II), trans. Francis Clarck Murgotten. New York: Columbia University.

Barceló, Miquel (1986), 'Vespres del feudals.' In J. Portella i Comas (ed.), *La formacio i expansio del feudalisme catala. Homenatge a Santiago Sobreques i Vidal*, pp. 237–49. Girona: Universitat de Girona.

Barceló, Miquel (ed.) (1997), *El Sol que salió por occidente (Estudios sobre el estado omeya en al-Andalus)*. Jaén: Universidad de Jaén.

Barceló, Miquel, Kirchner, Helena and Navarro, Carmen (eds) (1996), *El agua que no duerme. Fundamentos de la arqueología hidraúlica andalusí*. Granada: El Legado Andalusí.

Barrett, John (2014), 'The Material Constitution of Humanness.' *Archaeological Dialogues* 21.1: 65–74.

Bateson, Gregory (2002), *Mind and Nature: A Necessary Unity*. New Jersey: Hampton Press.

Bennett, Jane (2010), *Vibrant Matter: A Political Ecology of Things*. London: Duke University Press.

De Beylié, Leon (1909), *La Kalaa des Beni-Hammad. Une Capitale Berebère de l'Afrique du Nord au XIe Siècle*. Paris: Ernest Leroux.

Bhabha, Homi (1994), *The Location of Culture*. London and New York: Routledge.

Bloch, Maurice (2012), *Anthropology and the Cognitive Challenge*. Cambridge: Cambridge University Press.

Bonnéric, Julie (2020), 'The Early Islamic Pottery from the Monastery at al-Qusur.' *Journal of Islamic Archaeology* 7 (1): 21–38.

Bonnéric, Julie (2021), 'Archaeological Evidence of an Early Islamic Monastery in the Centre of al-Qusur (Failaka Island, Kuwait).' *Arabian Archaeology and Epigraphy* 32 (1): 50–61.

Boone, James (2009), *Lost Civilization: The Contested Islamic Past in Spain and Portugal*. London: Duckworth.

Bourdieu, Pierre (1977) [1972], *Outline of a Theory of Practice*, trans. Richard Nice. Cambridge: Cambridge University Press.

Bourdieu, Pierre (1990) [1980], *The Logic of Practice*, trans. Richard Nice. Stanford: Stanford University Press.

Bulliet, Richard (1979), *Conversion to Islam in the Medieval Period. An Essay in Quantitative History*. Cambridge MA and London: Harvard University Press.

Cantwell Smith, Wilfred (1963), *The Meaning and End of Religion*. New York: MacMillan.

Cantwell Smith, Wilfred (1981), *On Understanding Islam: Selected Studies*. The Hague: Mouton Publishers.

De Cardi, Beatrice (1978), 'Gazetteer of Sites and Finds.' In Beatrice De Cardi (ed.), *Qatar Archaeological Report. Excavations 1973*, pp. 181–200. Oxford: Oxford University Press and Qatar National Museum.

Carlson, Thomas A. (2015), 'Contours of Conversion. The Geography of Islamization in Syria 600–1500.' *Journal of the American Oriental Society* 135 (4): 791–816.

Carpio Dueñas, Juan, García Sanjuán, Alejandro and Mayor Zaragoza, Federico (2018), *Informe. Comisión de Expertos Sobre la Mezquita Catedral de Córdoba*. Report submitted to the Town Council of Cordoba (Spain). Available online: https://unescoandalucia.org/blog/informe-de-lacomision-de-expertos-sobre-la-mezquita-catedral-de-cordoba, last accessed 22 August 2022.

Carter, Robert (2013), 'Christianity in the Gulf During the First Centuries of Islam.' *Arabian Archaeology and Epigraphy* 19 (1): 71–108.

Carter, Robert and Naranjo Santana, Javier (2011), *Muharraq Excavations 2010*. Report submitted to the Ministry of Culture and Information of Bahrain.

Carter, Robert and Stremke, Frank (2021), *Landscapes of Faith. Aerial Survey of 7th-9th Century Sites of North Qatar*. Report presented to Qatar Museums, Doha.

Carvajal López, José C. (2008), *La Cerámica de Madīnat Ilbīra (Atarfe) y el Poblamiento Altomedieval de la Vega de Granada*. Granada: THARG.

Carvajal López, José C. (2009), 'Pottery Production and Islam in South-East Spain: A Social Model.' *Antiquity* 83: 388–98.

Carvajal López, José C. (2012), 'Cooking Pots and Large Containers in the Early Medieval Vega of Granada (South East Spain). On the Practices of Pottery Production and the Practices that Require Production of Pottery.' *The Old Potter's Almanach* 17 (2): 7–12.

Carvajal López, José C. (2013), 'Islamicization or Islamicizations? Expansion of Islam and Social Practice in the Vega of Granada (South-East Spain).' *World Archaeology* 45 (1): 56–70.

Carvajal López, José C. (2014), 'The Archaeology of al-Andalus. Past, Present and Future.' *Medieval Archaeology* 58: 318–39.

Carvajal López, José C. (2017), 'Islamization and Trade in the Arabian Gulf in the Age of Mohammad and Charlemagne.' In John Mitchell, John Moreland and Beatrice Leal (eds), *Encounters, Excavations and Argosies. Essays for Richard Hodges*, pp. 73–90. Oxford: Archaeopress.

Carvajal López, José C. (2019), 'After the Conquest: Ceramics and Migrations.' *Journal of Medieval Iberian Studies* 11 (3): 323–41.

Carvajal López, José C. (2020a), 'Landscapes of Water and Landscapes of Power: Hydraulic Politics in Butrint (Albania) between Venetians and Ottomans.' *Levant* 51 (2): 184–200.

Carvajal López, José C. (2020b), 'Material Culture,' In Maribel Fierro Bello (ed.), *The Routledge Handbook of Muslim Iberia*, pp. 486–512. London and New York: Routledge.

Carvajal López, José C. (2021), 'Long Term Patterns of Nomadic and Sedentary Settlement in the Crowded Desert of North-West Qatar.' In Piers Dixon and Claudia Theune (eds), *Ruralia XIII: Seasonal Settlement in the*

Medieval and Early Modern Countryside, pp. 285-94. Leiden: Sidestone Press.

Carvajal López, José C. (2022), 'Sobre cerámica, cambio tecnológico e islamización.' In Eneko Lopez Martínez de Marigorta (ed.), *Una Nueva Mirada a Al-Andalus. Retos de la Investigación Arqueológica y Textual del Periodo Omeya*, pp. 77-95. Documentos de Arqueología Medieval 18. Vitoria: Editorial Universidad del País Vasco.

Carvajal López, José C. (forthcoming), 'Islamization and Ceramics. Assembling Change and Con-Text.' In Joanita Vroom and Hagit Nol (eds.), *Material Entanglements in the Islamic World. New Approaches to Islamic Archaeology and Ceramics*. Turnhout: Brepols.

Carvajal López, José C., and Day, Peter M. (2013), 'Cooking Pots and Islamicization in the Early Medieval Vega of Granada (Al-Andalus, Sixth to Twelfth Centuries).' *Oxford Journal of Archaeology* 32 (4): 433-51.

Carvajal López, José C., and Day, Peter M. (2015), 'The Production and Distribution of Cooking Pots in Two Towns of South East Spain in the 6th-11th Centuries.' *Journal of Archaeological Science. Reports* 2: 282-90.

Carvajal López, José Cristobal, Hayden, Benen, Alexiou, Konstantinos and García, Marcos (2011), *Field Report on Venetian-Ottoman Survey Carried Out in July 2010 and March 2011*. Unpublished report presented to The Butrint Foundation.

Carvajal López, José C. and Palanco Noguerol, Ana (2013), 'The Castle of Ali Pasha at Butrint.' In Inge Lyse Hansen, Richard Hodges and Sarah Leppard (eds), *Butrint 4. The Archaeology and Histories of an Ionian Town*, pp. 289-308. Oxford: Oxbow Books.

Carvajal López, José C., Morabito, Laura, Carter, Robert, Fletcher, Richard and Al-Naʻīmī, Faisal A. (2016), 'The Crowded Desert: A Multi-Phase Archaeological Survey in the North-West of Qatar.' *Proceedings of the Seminar for Arabian Studies* 46: 45-62.

Carvajal López, José C. and Jiménez Puertas, Miguel (2017), 'Cuisine, Islamisation and Ceramics in the South and East of Al-Andalus.' In Joanita Vroom, Yona Waksman and Roos van Oosten (eds), *Medieval MasterChef. Archaeological and Historical Perspectives on Eastern Cuisine and Western Foodways*, pp. 33-62, 371. Turnhout: Brepols.

Carvajal López, José C., Roberts, Kirk, Rees, Gareth, Stremke, Frank, Marsh, Anke, Morabito, Laura, Bevan, Andrew, Altaweel, Mark, Harrison, Rodney, Arroyo-Kalin, Manuel, Carter, Robert, Fletcher, Richard and Al-Naʻīmī,

Faisal (2017), 'A Crowded Desert: Early Results from Survey and Excavation of Nomadic Sites in North-West Qatar.' *Proceedings of the Seminar for Arabian Studies* 47: 43–50.

Carvajal López, José C., Hein, Anno, Glascock, Michael and Day, Peter M. (2018), 'Combined Petrographic and Chemical Analysis of Water Containers and Glazed Wares in the Early Islamic Vega of Granada (Southeast Spain, 6th to 12th Centuries CE).' *Journal of Archaeological Science. Reports* 21: 1130–40.

Carvajal López, José C., Roberts, Kirk, Morabito, Laura, Rees, Gareth, Stremke, Frank, Marsh, Anke, Carter, Robert and Al-Naʿīmī, Faisal A. (2018), 'From Tentscape to Landscape. A Multi-Scale Analysis of Long-Term Patterns of Occupation in North-West Qatar.' *Proceedings of the Seminar for Arabian Studies* 48: 31–45.

Carvajal López, José C., Roberts, Kirk, Morabito, Laura, Rees, Gareth, Stremke, Frank, Marsh, Anke, Freire-Lista, David, Carter, Robert and Al-Naʿīmī, Faisal A. (2020), 'The Dawn of the Islamic era? The Excavation of Yughbī in the Crowded Desert of Qatar.' *Proceedings of the Seminar for Arabian Studies* 50: 53–69.

Carvajal López, José C., Živković, Jelena, Aljawabra, Alkindi and Lababidi, Rim (2020), 'Islamic Heritage in Three Peninsulas: Qatar, Iberia, and the Balkans.' In Bethany Walker, Timothy Insoll and Corisande Fenwick (eds), *The Oxford Handbook of Islamic Archaeology*, pp. 731–54. Oxford: Oxford University Press.

Castillo Armenteros, Juan C. (1998), *La Campiña de Jaén en Época Emiral (Siglos VIII–X)*. Jaén: Universidad de Jaén.

Chaudhuri, Kirti N. (1985), *Trade and Civilisation in the Indian Ocean: An Economic History from the Rise of Islam to 1750*. Cambridge: Cambridge University Press.

Cipolla, Craig N. (2020), 'Discussing Different Pasts.' In Rachel J. Crellin, Craig N. Cipolla, Lindsay M. Montgomery, Oliver J. T. Harris, Sophie V. Moore (eds), *Archaeological Theory in Dialogue. Situating Relationality, Ontology, Posthumanism, and Indigenous Paradigms*, pp. 151–67. London and New York: Routledge.

Conlin Casella, Eleanor and Fowler, Chris (eds) (2005), *The Archaeology of Plural and Changing Identities*. New York: Kluwer Academic/Plenum Publishers.

Conneller, Chantal (2011), *An Archaeology of Materials: Substantial Transformations in Early Prehistoric Europe*. London and New York: Routledge.

Conneller, Chantal (2017), 'Commentary: Materializing Assemblages.' *Cambridge Archaeological Journal* 27 (1): 183–5.
Crellin, Rachel J. (2017), 'Changing Assemblages: Vibrant Matter in Burial Assemblages.' *Cambridge Archaeological Journal* 27 (1): 111–25.
Crellin, Rachel J. (2020), *Change and Archaeology*. London and New York: Routledge.
Crellin, Rachel J., Cipolla, Craig N., Montgomery, Lindsay M., Harris, Oliver J. T., Moore, Sophie V. (2020), *Archaeological Theory in Dialogue. Situating Relationality, Ontology, Posthumanism, and Indigenous Paradigms*. London and New York: Routledge.
Crone, Patricia (1980), *Slaves on Horses. The Evolution of the Islamic Polity*. Cambridge: Cambridge University Press.
al-Dailami, Ahmed (2014), '"Purity and confusion": The Hawala between Persians and Arabs in the Contemporary Gulf.' In Lawrence G. Potter (ed.), *The Persian Gulf in Modern Times. People, Ports and History*, pp. 299–326. New York: Palgrave MacMillan.
Damásio, António (2000), *The Feeling of What Happens. Body and Emotion and the Making of Consciousness*. London: Vintage.
Davies, Siriol (2013), 'Late Venetian Butrint: 16th–18th centuries.' In Inge Lyse Hansen, Richard Hodges and Sarah Leppard (eds), *Butrint 4. The Archaeology and Histories of an Ionian Town*, pp. 280–8. Oxford: Oxbow Books.
DeLanda, Manuel (2006), *A New Philosophy of Society. Assemblage Theory and Social Complexity*. London: Bloomsbury.
DeLanda, Manuel (2016), *Assemblage Theory*. Edinburgh: Edinburgh University Press.
Deleuze, Gilles (1990 [1969]), *The Logic of Sense*, trans. Mark Lester with Charles Stivale. London: The Athlone Press.
Deleuze, Gilles (1994 [1968]), *Difference and Repetition*, trans. Paul Patton. New York: Columbia University Press.
Deleuze, Gilles and Guattari, Felix (1983 [1977]), *Anti-Oedipus: Capitalism and Schizophrenia*, trans. Robert Hurley, Mark Seem and Helen R. Lane. Minneapolis: University of Minnesota Press.
Deleuze, Gilles and Guattari, Felix (1987 [1980]), *A Thousand Plateaus. Capitalism and Schizophrenia*, trans. Brian Massumi. Minneapolis: University of Minnesota Press.
DeWeese, Devin (1995), *Islamization and Native Religion in the Golden Horde: Baba Tükles and Conversion to Islam in Historical and Epic Tradition*. University Park: Pennsylvania State University Press.

Díaz-Andreu, Margarita (1996), 'Islamic Archaeology and the Origin of the Spanish Nation.' In Margarita Díaz-Andreu and Timothy Champion (eds), *Nationalism and Archaeology in Europe*, pp. 68–89. London: UCL Press.

Doja, Albert (2004), 'Spiritual Surrender: From Companionship to Hierarchy in the History of Bektashism.' *Numen* 53 (4): 448–510.

Donaldson, William J. (1979), *Fishing and Fish Marketing in Northern Oman. A Case Study of Artisanal Fisheries Development*. PhD diss., University of Durham, Durham.

Donner, Fred M. (1981), *The Early Islamic Conquests*. Princeton: Princeton University Press.

Donner, Fred M. (2010), *Muhammad and the Believers: At the Origins of Islam*. Cambridge MA: Belknap Press-Harvard University Press.

Eaton, Richard M. (1993), *The Rise of Islam and the Bengal Frontier 1204–1760*. Berkeley: University of California Press.

Encyclopaedia of Islam, Second Edition (1960–2005), Edited by P. Bearman, Th. Bianquis, C. E. Bosworth, E. van Donzel, W. P. Heinrichs. Leiden: Brill.

Fabietti, Ugo (2012), 'Errancy in Ethnography and Theory. On the Meaning and Role of "Discovery" in Anthropological Research.' In H. Hazam and E. Herzog (eds), *Serendipity in Archaeological Research. The Nomadic Turn*, pp. 15–30. London and New York: Routledge.

Fenwick, Corisande (2019), *Early Islamic North Africa. A New Perspective*. London: Bloomsbury.

Fernández Navarro, Esteban (2008), *Tradicion Tecnological de la Ceramica de Cocina Almohade-Nazari en la Provincia de Granada*. Granada: THARG.

Fisher, Humphrey J. (1973), 'Conversions Reconsidered: Some Historical Aspects of Religious Conversion in Black Africa.' *Africa* 43: 27–40.

Fisher, Humphrey J. (1985), 'The Juggernaut's Apologia: Conversion to Islam in Black Africa.' *Africa* 55: 153–73.

Flecker, Michael (2011), 'A Ninth-Century Arab Shipwreck in Indonesia. The First Archaeological Evidence of Direct Trade with China.' In Regina Krahl, John Guy, R. Keith Wilson and Julian Raby (eds), *Shipwrecked. Tang Treasures and Monsoon Winds*, pp. 101–9. Singapore: Smithsonian Institution – National Heritage Board, Singapore.

Fleisher, Jeffrey (2019), 'The Gathering of Swahili Religious Practice: Mosques-as-Assemblages at 1000 CE Swahili Towns.' In Susan M. Alt and Timothy R. Pauketat (eds), *New Materialisms Ancient Urbanisms*, pp. 158–83. London and New York: Routledge.

Fowler, Chris (2004), *The Archaeology of Personhood: An Anthropological Approach*. London and New York: Routledge.

Fowler, Chris (2013), *The Emergent Past: A Relational Realist Archaeology of Early Bronze Age Mortuary Practices*. Oxford: Oxford University Press.

Fowler, Chris (2017), 'Relational Typologies, Assemblage Theory and Early Bronze Age Burials.' *Cambridge Archaeological Journal* 27 (1): 95–109.

Gabriel, Albert (1920), 'Les fouilles de Foustat.' *Comptes Rendus des Séances de l'Académie des Inscriptions et Belles-Lettres, 64e année*, 3: 243–7.

Gachet-Bizollon, Jacqueline (ed.) (2011), *Le Tell d'Akkaz au Kuweït – Tell Akkaz in Kuwait*. Travaux de la Maison de l'Orient et de la Méditerranée 57. Lyon: Maison de l'Orient et de la Méditerranée.

García Sanjuán, Alejandro (2012), 'Al-Andalus en la historiografía del nacionalismo españolista. Entre la España musulmana y la Reconquista (siglos XIX–XXI).' In D. Melo Carrasco and F. Vidal Castro (eds), *A 1300 años de la conquista de Al-Andalus*, pp. 65–104. Coquimbo: Centro Mohamed VI para el Diálogo entre las Civilizaciones.

García, Marcos (2019), *Explotación y Consumo de los Animales en el Sudeste de la Península Ibérica durante la Alta Edad Media (ss. VII–X). Perspectivas Históricas y Zooarqueológicas*. PhD diss., University of Granada, Granada.

Geertz, Clifford (1968), *Islam Observed: Religious Development in Morocco and Indonesia*. Chicago and London: The University of Chicago Press.

Geertz, Clifford (1973), *The Interpretation of Culture*. New York: Basic Books.

Gellner, Ernest (1981), *Muslim Society*. Cambridge, Cambridge University Press.

George, Alan (2015), 'Direct Sea Trade between Early Islamic Iraq and Tang China: From the Exchange of Goods to the Transmission of Ideas.' *Journal of the Royal Asiatic Society* 25: 579–624.

Giddens, Anthony (1984), *The Constitution of Society*. Cambridge: Polity Press.

Glick, Thomas F. (1995), *From Muslim Fortress to Christian Castle: Social and Cultural Change in Medieval Spain*. Manchester: Manchester University Press.

Gómez Becerra, Antonio (1998), *El Poblamiento Altomedieval en la Costa de Granada*. Granada: THARG.

Gómez Moreno, Manuel (1898), *Medina Elvira*. Granada: Imprenta La Lealtad.

Gosselain, Olivier (1998), 'Social and Technical Identity in a Clay Crystal Ball.' In Miriam T. Stark (ed.), *The Archaeology of Social Boundaries*, pp. 78–106. Washington: The Smithsonian Institution.

Gosselain, Olivier (2000), 'Materializing Identities: An African Perspective.' *Journal of Archaeological Method and Theory* 7: 187–217.

Gosselain, Olivier (2008), 'Thoughts and Adjustments in the Potter's Backyard.' In Ina Berg (ed.), *Breaking the Mould: Challenging the Past through Pottery* (BAR International Series S1861 and Prehistoric Ceramics Research Group: Occasional Paper 6), pp. 67–79. Oxford: Archaeopress.

Gosselain, Olivier (2010), 'Exploring the Dynamics of African Pottery Cultures.' In Randi Barndon, Asbjørn Engevik and Ingvild Øye (eds), *The Archaeology of Regional Technologies. Case Studies from the Palaeolithic to the Age of the Vikings*, pp. 193–224. Lewiston NY: Edwin Mellen Press.

Grabar, Oleg (1971), 'Islamic Archaeology: An Introduction.' *Archaeology* 24 (3): 196–9.

Grabar, Oleg (1976), 'Islamic Art and Archaeology.' In Leonard Binder (ed.), *The Study of the Middle East*, pp. 229–63. New York: John Wiley.

Grafman, Rafi and Myriam Rosen-Ayalon (1999), 'The Two Great Syrian Umayyad Mosques: Jerusalem and Damascus.' *Muqarnas: An Annual on the Visual Culture of the Islamic World* XVI: 1–15.

Guérin, Alexandrine and Al-Naʿīmī, Faisal A. (2009), 'Territory and Settlement Patterns During the Abbasid Period (Ninth Century AD): The Village of Murwab (Qatar).' *Proceedings of the Seminar of Arabian Studies* 39: 181–96.

Guérin, Alexandrine and Al-Naʿīmī, Faisal A. (2010), 'Preliminary Pottery Study: Murwab Horizon in Progress, Ninth century AD, Qatar.' *Proceedings of the Seminar of Arabian Studies* 40: 17–34.

Guerin, Orla (2020), 'Hagia Sophia: Turkey turns iconic Istanbul museum into mosque.' *BBC News*, 10 July 2020. Available online: https://www.bbc.co.uk/news/world-europe-53366307, visited on 22 August 2024.

Guichard, Pierre (1976), *Al-Andalus: Estructura antropológica de una sociedad islámica en Occidente*. Barcelona: Barral.

Gutiérrez Lloret, Sonia (1996), *La cora de Tudmir. De la antigüedad tardía al mundo islámico. Poblamiento y cultura material*. Madrid: Casa de Velázquez, Instituto de Cultura Juan Gil-Albert.

Gutiérrez Lloret, Sonia (2007), 'La islamización de Tudmir: balance y perspectivas.' In Philippe Sénac (coord.), *Villes et campagnes de Tarraconaise et d'al-Andalus (VIe-XIe siècles). La transition*, pp. 275–318. Toulouse: Université de Toulouse II – Le Mirail-CNRS.

Gutiérrez Lloret, Sonia (2012), 'La arqueología en la historia del temprano al-Andalus. Espacios sociales, cerámica e islamización.' In Philippe Sénac (coord.), *Histoire et archéologie de l'Occident musulman (VIIe-XVe siècles):*

Al-Andalus, Maghreb, Sicile, pp. 33–66. Toulouse: Université de Toulouse II – Le Mirail-CNRS.

Haiman, Mordechai (1995), 'Agriculture and Nomad-State Relations in the Negev Desert in the Byzantine and Early Islamic Periods.' *Bulletin of the American Schools of Oriental Research* 297: 29–53.

Haldon, John (1997), *The State and the Tributary Mode of Production*. London: Verso Books.

Hamilakis, Yannis (2017), 'Sensorial Assemblages: Affect, Memory and Temporality in Assemblage Thinking.' *Cambridge Archaeological Journal* 27 (1): 169–82.

Harman, Graham (2008), 'DeLanda's Ontology: Assemblage and Realism.' *Continental Philosophy Review* 41: 367–83.

Harris, Oliver J. T. (2014), '(Re)assembling Communities.' *Journal of Archaeological Method and Theory* 21: 76–97.

Harris, Oliver J. T. (2017), 'Assemblages and Scale in Archaeology.' *Cambridge Archaeological Journal* 27 (1): 127–39.

Harris, Oliver J. T. (2018), 'More than Representation: Multiscalar Assemblages and the Deleuzian Challenge to Archaeology.' *History of the Human Sciences* 31 (3): 83–104.

Harris, Oliver J. T. (2021), *Assembling Past Worlds. Materials, Bodies and Architecture in Neolithic Britain*. London and New York: Routledge.

Harris, Oliver J. T. and Cipolla, Craig N. (2017), *Archaeology in the New Millennium. Introducing Current Perspectives*. London and New York: Routledge.

Haw, Stephen G. (2017), 'The Maritime Routes between China and the Indian Ocean During the Second to Ninth Centuries CE.' *Journal of the Royal Asiatic Society of Great Britain and Ireland* 27 (1): 53–81.

Hillenbrand, Robert (1982), '*La dolce vita* in Early Islamic Syria: The Evidence of Later Umayyad Palaces.' *Art History* 5 (1): 1–35.

Hodder, Ian (2012), *Entangled: An Archaeology of the Relationships between Humans and Things*. Oxford: Wiley-Blackwell.

Hodder, Ian (2016), *Studies in Human-Thing Entanglement*. Stanford: Self-published.

Hodgson, Marshall G. S. (1974), *The Venture of Islam: Conscience and History in a World Civilization* (3 Vols). Chicago: The University of Chicago Press.

Holes, Clive D. (2011), 'Language and Identity in the Arabian Gulf.' *Journal of Arabian Studies* 1: 129–45.

Horton, Robin (1971), 'African Conversion.' *Africa* 41: 85–108.
Horton, Robin (1975), 'On the Rationality of Conversion.' *Africa* 45: 219–35.
Horton, Robin (1993), *Patterns of Thought in Africa and the West: Essays on Magic, Religion and Science*. Cambridge: Cambridge University Press.
Hourani, George (1979) [1951], *Arab Seafaring*. Princeton: Princeton University Press.
Hoyland, Robert (1997), *Seeing Islam as Others Saw It: A Survey and Evaluation of Christian, Jewish and Zoroastrian Writings on Early Islam*. Studies in Late Antiquity and Early Islam 13. Princeton NJ: The Darwin Press.
Hoyland, Robert (2006), 'New Documentary Texts and the Early Islamic State.' *Bulletin of the School of Oriental and African Studies* 69 (3): 395–416.
Hughes, Joe (2009), *Deleuze's 'Difference and Repetition': A Reader's Guide*. London: Bloomsbury.
Huntington, Samuel (1996), *The Clash of Civilizations and the Remaking of World Order*. London and New York: Simon and Schuster.
Ibn Hawqāl [Ibn Hawqāl abu-l-Qāsim Ibn Hawqāl al-Niṣibī] (1992), *Kitāb Sūrat al-Arḍ*. Beyrut, Dār Maktaba al-Ḥayah.
Ibn Ḥayyān [Abū Marwān Ḥayyān ibn Khalaf, al-maʿrūf bi Ibn Ḥayyān] (1937), *Al-Muktabis III*, ed. Melchor Antuña. Paris: Librairie Orientaliste.
Ibn Ḥayyān [Abū Marwān Ḥayyān ibn Khalaf, al-maʿrūf bi Ibn Ḥayyān] (1952), '*Al-Muqtabis* de Ibn Hayyan,' trans. José Guraieb. *Cuadernos de Historia de España* XVIII: 150–60.
Ingold, Tim (2007), 'Materials Against Materiality.' *Archaeological Dialogues* 14 (1): 1–16.
Ingold, Tim (2011), *Being Alive: Essays on Movement, Knowledge and Description*. London and New York: Routledge.
Inskip, Sarah (2013a), 'Islam in Iberia or Iberian Islam: Bioarchaeology and the Analysis of Emerging Islamic Identity in Early Medieval Iberia.' *Post-Classical Archaeologies* 3: 63–93.
Inskip, Sarah (2013b), *Islam in Iberia or Iberian Islam: Sociobioarchaeology and the Analysis of Emerging Islamic Identity in Early Medieval Iberia*. PhD diss., University of Southampton. Southampton.
Insoll, Timothy (1996), *Islam, Archaeology and History: Gao Region (Mali), ca. AD 900–1250*. Cambridge Monographs in African Archaeology 39; British Archaeological Reports International Series 647. Oxford: British Archaeological Reports.

Insoll, Timothy (1999), *The Archaeology of Islam*. Oxford: Wiley-Blackwell.

Insoll, Timothy (2003), *The Archaeology of Islam in Sub-Saharan Africa*. Cambridge: Cambridge University Press.

Insoll, Timothy (2004), *Archaeology, Ritual, Religion*. London and New York: Routledge.

Insoll, Timothy (ed.) (2005), *The Land of Enki in the Islamic Era. Pearls, Palms and Religious Identity in Bahrain*. London: Kegan Paul.

Insoll, Timothy (ed.) (2007), *The Archaeology of Identities: A Reader*. London and New York: Routledge.

Insoll, Timothy (2015), *Material Explorations in African Archaeology*. Oxford: Oxford University Press.

Insoll, Timothy (2016), 'The Archaeology of Islamisation in Sub-Saharan Africa: A Comparative Study.' In Andrew Peacock (ed.), *Islamisation. Comparative Perspectives from History*, pp. 244–73. Edinburgh: Edinburgh University Press.

Insoll, Timothy (2017), 'First Footsteps in the Archaeology of Harar, Ethiopia.' *Journal of Islamic Archaeology* 4 (2): 189–215.

Insoll, Timothy (2020), 'The Islamic Archaeology of Ethiopia and the Horn of Africa.' In Bethany Walker, Timothy Insoll and Corisande Fenwick (eds), *The Oxford Handbook of Islamic Archaeology*, pp. 417–45. Oxford: Oxford University Press.

Insoll, Timothy, Carter, Robert, Almahari, Salman and MacLean, Rachel (2021a), 'Excavations at Samahij, Bahrain, and the Implications of Christianity, Islamisation and settlement in Bahrain.' *Arabian Archaeology and Epigraphy* 32 (S1): 395–421.

Insoll, Timothy, Khalaf, Nadia, MacLean, Rachel, Parsons-Morgan, Hannah, Tait, Nicholas, Gaastra, Jane, Beldados, Alemseged, Pryor, Alexander J. E., Evis, Laura and Dussubieuz, Laure (2021b), 'Material Cosmopolitanism: The Entrepot of Harlaa as an Islamic Gateway to Eastern Ethiopia.' *Antiquity* 95 (380): 487–507.

Iqbal, Muzaffar (ed.) (2012), *Studies in the Making of Islamic Science: Knowledge in Motion*. Islam and Science: Historic and Contemporary Perspectives, vol 4. Farnham: Ashgate.

al-Istakhrī [Abū Ishāk al-Farsī al-Istakhrī] (1927): *Kitāb al-Masālik wa-l-Mamālik*, ed. M. J. De Goeje. Leiden: Brill.

Jansen van Rensburg, Julian (2016), *The Maritime Traditions of the Fishermen of Socotra, Yemen*. Oxford: Archaeopress.

Jervis, Ben (2017a), 'Assembling the Archaeology of the Global Middle Ages.' *World Archaeology* 49 (5): 666–80.

Jervis, Ben (2017b), 'Assessing Urban Fortunes in Six Late Medieval Ports: An Archaeological Application of Assemblage Theory.' *Urban History* 44 (1): 2–26.

Jervis, Ben (2018), *Assemblage Thought and Archaeology*. London and New York: Routledge.

Jiménez Puertas, Miguel and Carvajal López, José C. (2011), 'Opciones sociotécnicas de regadío y secano. El caso de la Vega de Granada.' In Flocel Sabaté (ed.), *Els espais del secà. Actas del IV Curs d'Arqueologia Medieval. Lleida-Algerri, 12–13 Març 2009*, pp. 51–85. Lleida, Universitat de Lleida.

Jiménez Puertas, Miguel and Carvajal López, José C. (2020), 'La cerámica altomedieval de El Castillejo de Nívar (siglos VI-XII) y su contexto económico-social.' In Antonio Malpica Cuello and Alberto García Porras (eds), *Cerámica medieval e historia económico-social: problemas de método y casos de estudio*, pp. 15–44. Granada, THARG.

Johns, Jeremy (1999), 'The "House of the Prophet" and the Concept of the Mosque.' In Jeremy Johns (ed.), *Bayt al-Maqdis II: Jerusalem and Early Islam*. Oxford Studies in Islamic Art 9. Oxford: Oxford University Press.

Johns, Jeremy (2003), 'Archaeology and the History of Early Islam.' *Journal of the Social and Economic History of the Orient* 46 (4): 411–36.

Jones, Jude (2017), 'Being, Belief, Comprehension and Confusion: An Exploration of the Assemblages of English Post-Reformation Parochial Religion.' *Cambridge Archaeological Journal* 27 (1): 141–54.

Jones, Siân (1997), *The Archaeology of Ethnicity*. London and New York: Routledge.

Kennedy, Hugh (2010), 'The City and the Nomad.' In Robert Irwin (ed), *The New Cambridge History of Islam Vol. 4: Islamic Cultures and Societies to the End of the Eighteenth Century*, pp. 274–89. Cambridge: Cambridge University Press.

Kennedy, Hugh (2014), 'The Feeding of the Five Hundred Thousand: Cities and Agriculture in Early Islamic Mesopotamia.' *Iraq* 73: 177–99.

Kennet, Derek (2004), *Sasanian and Islamic Pottery from Ra's al-Khaimah: Classification, Chronology and Analysis of Trade in the Western Indian Ocean*. (British Archaeological Reports, International Series, 1248). Oxford: Archaeopress.

Kennet, Derek (2012), 'Archaeological History of the Northern Emirates in the Islamic Period: An outline.' In Daniel T. Potts and Peter Hellyer (eds), *Fifty*

Years of Emirates Archaeology, pp. 189–201. Abu Dhabi: Motivate Publishing.

Kennet, Derek, Ulrich, Brian and Le Maguer, Sterenn (2013), *Kadhima: Kuwait in the Early Centuries of Islam*. Kuwait: National Council for Culture, Arts and Letters.

King, Geoffrey (1997), 'The History of the UAE: The Eve of Islam and the Islamic Period.' In Edmund Ghareeb and Ibrahim Al Abed (eds), *Perspectives on the United Arab Emirates*, pp. 74–94. London: Trident Press.

Kirchner, Helena (2009), 'Original Design, Tribal Management and Modifications in Medieval Hydraulic Systems in the Balearic Islands (Spain).' *World Archaeology* 41 (1): 151–68.

Lape, Peter V. (2000), 'Political Dynamics and Religious Change in the Late Pre-Colonial Banda Islands, Eastern Indonesia.' *World Archaeology* 32 (1): 138–55.

Latour, Bruno (1993) [1991], *We Have Never Been Modern*, trans. C. Porter. Cambridge, MA: Harvard University Press.

Levtzion, Nehemia (1973), *Ancient Ghana and Mali*. London: Methuen.

Levtzion, Nehemia, ed. (1979), *Conversion to Islam*. New York and London: Holems and Meier Publishers.

Lic, Agniezska (2017), 'Chronology of Stucco Production in the Persian-Arab Gulf and Mesopotamia in the Early Islamic Period.' *Proceedings of the Seminar for Arabian Studies* 47: 151–62.

López Martínez de Marigorta, Eneko (2020), *Mercaderes, Artesanos y Ulemas. Las Ciudades de las Coras de Ilbīra y Pechina en Época Omeya*. Jaén: Universidad de Jaén.

Lucas Gavin (2012), *Understanding the Archaeological Record*. Cambridge: Cambridge University Press.

Lucas, Gavin (2017), 'Variations on a Theme: Assemblage Archaeology.' *Cambridge Archaeological Journal* 27 (1): 187–90.

Macumber, Phillip (2016), 'The Islamic Occupation of Qatar in the Context of an Environmental Framework.' In Stephen McPhillips and Paul Wordsworth (eds), *Landscapes of the Islamic World: Archaeology, History and Ethnography*, pp. 34–49. Philadelphia: Pennsylvania University Press.

Magness, Jodi (1993), *Jerusalem Ceramic Chronology: circa 200–800 CE*. Sheffield: Sheffield Academic Press.

Magness, Jodi (2003), *The Archaeology of the Early Islamic Settlement in Palestine*. Winona Lake, NI: Eisenbrauns.

Mahias, Marie-Claude (1993), 'Pottery Techniques in India.' In Pierre Lemmonier (ed.), *Technological Choices. Transformation in Material Cultures since the Neolithic*, pp. 157–80. London and New York: Routledge.

Makharadze, Zurab, Kvirkvelia, Guram, Murvanidze, Bidzina, Chkhvimiani, Jimsher, Ad Duweish, Sultan, Al Mutairi, Hamed and Lordkipanidze, David (2017), 'Kuwait-Georgian Archaeological Mission – Archaeological Investigations on the Island of Failaka in 2011–2017.' *Bulletin of the Georgian National Academy of Sciences* 11 (4): 177–86.

Manzano Moreno, Eduardo (2006), *Conquistadores, Emires y Califas. Los Omeyas y la Formacion de al-Andalus*. Barcelona: Crítica.

Marranci, Gabriele (2006), *Jihad Beyond Islam*. Oxford and New York: Berg.

Marranci, Gabriele (2008), *The Anthropology of Islam*. Oxford and New York: Berg.

Martínez Enamorado, Virgilio (2003), *Al-Andalus desde la Periferia. La Formación de una Sociedad Musulmana en Tierras Malagueñas (siglos VIII–X)*. Málaga: Diputación de Málaga.

al-Masʿūdī [Abu-l-Ḥassan ʿAlī ibn al-Ḥusayn ibn ʿAlī al-Masʿūdī] (1861–7): *Les Prairies d'Or* (vol I), trans. C. Barbier de Maeillart and A. Pavet de Courteille. Paris: L'Imprimerie Imperiale.

McPhillips, Stephen, Rosendahl, Sandra and Morgan, Victoria (2015), 'Abbasid Rural Settlement in Northern Qatar: Seasonal Tribal Exploitation of an Arid Environment?' *Proceedings of the Seminar of Arabian Studies* 45: 185–98.

Meirion Jones, Andrew (2017), 'The Art of Assemblage: Styling Neolithic Art.' *Cambridge Archaeological Journal* 27 (1): 85–94.

Meskell, Lynn (2002), 'The Intersections of Identity and Politics in Archaeology.' *Annual Review of Anthropology* 31: 279–301.

Di Miceli, Andrea (2021), 'The Site of Al-Qurainiyah: Topography and Phases of an Early Islamic Coastal Settlement on Failaka Island.' *Arabian Archaeology and Epigraphy* 32 (1): 62–9.

Milton, Kay (2005), 'Meanings, Feelings and Human Ecology.' In Kay Milton and Maruška Svašek (eds), *Mixed Emotions: Anthropological Studies of Feeling*, pp. 25–41. Oxford and New York: Berg.

Milwright, Marcus (2010), *An Introduction to Islamic Archaeology*. Edinburgh: Edinburgh University Press.

Molera, Judit, Carvajal López, José C., Molina, Glòria, and Pradell, Trinitat (2018), 'Glazes, Colorants and Decorations in Early Islamic Glazes from the Vega of Granada (9th to 12th centuries AD).' *Journal of Archaeological Science. Reports* 21: 1141–51.

Montgomery, Lindsay M. (2020), 'Indigenous Alterity as Archaeological Praxis.' In Rachel J. Crellin, Craig N. Cipolla, Lindsay M. Montgomery, Oliver J. T. Harris, Sophie V. Moore (eds), *Archaeological Theory in Dialogue. Situating Relationality, Ontology, Posthumanism, and Indigenous Paradigms*, pp. 51–66. London and New York: Routledge.

Mustafa, Mentor (2008), 'What Remained of Religion in an "Atheist" State and the Return of Religion in Post-Communist Albania.' In Jaka Repič, Alenka Bartulović and Katarina Sajovec Altshul (eds), *MESS and RAMSES II. Vol. 7, Mediterranean Ethnological Summer School*, pp. 51–76. Lubliana: Znanstvena Založba Filozofske Fakultete Univerze v Ljubljani.

Olsen, Bjørnard (2007), 'Keeping Things at an Arm's Length: A Genealogy of Symmetry.' *World Archaeology* 39: 579–88.

Olsen, Bjørnard (2010), *In Defence of Things: Archaeology and the Ontology of Objects*. Plymouth: Altamira Press.

Olsen, Bjørnard, Shanks, Michael, Webmoor, Timothy and Witmore, Christopher G. (2012), *Archaeology: The Discipline of Things*. Berkeley: University of California Press.

Parangoni, Ilir (2015), *Archaeological Survey of the St. Dimitri Hill, Butrint 2015*. Unpublished report presented to The Butrint Foundation, Norwich.

Pauketat, Timothy (2012), *An Archaeology of the Cosmos: Rethinking Agency and Religion in Ancient America*. London and New York: Routledge.

Peacock, Andrew C. S. (ed.) (2016a), *Islamisation: Comparative Perspectives from History*. Edinburgh: Edinburgh University Press.

Peacock, Andrew C. S. (2016b), 'Introduction.' In A. C. S. Peacock (ed.), *Islamisation: Comparative Perspectives from History*, pp. 1–18. Edinburgh: Edinburgh University Press.

Potter, Lawrence G. (1998), 'The Consolidation of Iran's Frontier on the Persian Gulf in the Nineteenth Century.' In Roxane Farmanfarmaian (ed.), *War and Peace in Qajar Persia. Implications, Past and Present*, pp. 125–48. London and New York: Routledge.

Power, Timothy (2009), 'The Expansion of Muslim Commerce in the Red Sea Basin, *c.* AD 833–969.' In Lucy Blue, John Cooper, Ross Thomas and Julian Whitewright (eds), *Connected Hinterlands. Proceedings of the Red Sea Project IV Held at the University of Southampton, September 2008*. BAR International Series 2052 / Society for Arabian Studies Monograph no. 8, pp. 111–18. Oxford: Archaeopress.

Priestman, Seth M. N. (2021), *Ceramic Exchange and the Indian Ocean Economy (AD 400–1275)* (2 Vols). British Museum Research Publications no. 223. London: The British Museum.

Rawlinson, Kevin (2018), 'Darren Osborne jailed for life for Finsbury Park attack.' *The Guardian*, 2 February 2018. Available online: https://www.theguardian.com/uk-news/2018/feb/02/finsbury-park-attack-darren-osborne-jailed, visited on 22 August 2024.

Ridgeway, William (1908), 'The Origin of the Turkish Crescent.' *The Journal of the Royal Anthropological Institute of Great Britain and Ireland* 38: 241–58.

Robb, John and Harris. Oliver J. T. (2013), *The Body in History: Europe from the Palaeolithic to the Future*. Cambridge: Cambridge University Press.

Robinson, Chase F. (2010), 'The Rise of Islam, 600–705.' In Chase F. Robinson (ed.), *The New Cambridge History of Islam, Vol. 1: The Formation of the Islamic World Sixth to Eleventh Centuries*, pp. 173–225. Cambridge: Cambridge University Press.

Román Punzón, Julio M. and Carvajal López, Jose C. (2018), 'Space, Shape and Recipe. Analysis of Cultural Change between the Late Antique and the Early Medieval Period in the Area of Granada in the Light of the Pottery of the Excavation of the Faculty of Economics in Granada (2011–2012).' In *¿Tipologías? Nuevas metodologías aplicadas. Algo más que galbos y cacharros. Etnoarqueología y experimentación cerámica. Menga Monografías 4*. pp. 493–507. Seville: Junta de Andalucía.

Roselló i Bordoy, Guillermo (1978), *Ensayo de sistematización de la cerámica árabe de Mallorca*. Diputación Provincial de Baleares, Instituto de Estudios Baleáricos, Consejo Superior de Investigaciones Científicas: Palma de Mallorca.

Ruthven, Malise (1997), *Islam: A Very Short Introduction*. Oxford: Oxford University Press.

Said, Edward (1978), *Orientalism*. New York: Vintage.

Salinas, Elena, Pradell, Trinitat, Matin, Moujan and Tite, Michael (2019), 'From Tin- to Antimony-Based Yellow Opacifiers in the Early Islamic Egyptian Glazes: Regional Influences and Ruling Dynasties.' *Journal of Archaeological Science: Reports* 26: 101923.

Sánchez Albornoz, Claudio (1956), *España, un enigma histórico*. Buenos Aires: Editorial Sudamericana.

Sarr Marrocco, Bilal (2011), *La Granada Zirí (1013–1090)*. Granada: Alhulia.

Sarre, Friedrich, and Herzfeld, Ersnt (1911–20), *Archäologische Reise im Euphrat- und Tigris-Gebiet* (4 Vols). Berlin: Verlag von Dietrich Reiner.

Sasaki, Tatsuo (1996), 'Umayyad and Abbasid finds from the 1994 excavations at Jazirat al-Hulayla.' *Bulletin of Archaeology, The University of Kanazawa* 23: 179–222.

Sasaki, Tatsuo and Sasaki, Hanae (1996), '1995 Excavations at Jazirat al-Hulayla.' *Bulletin of Archaeology, The University of Kanazawa* 23: 37–178.

Sasaki, Tatsuo and Sasaki, Hanae (1998), '1997 Excavations at Jazirat al-Hulayla, Ras Al-Khaimah, U.A.E.' *Bulletin of Archaeology, The University of Kanazawa* 24: 99–196.

Sasaki, Tatsuo and Sasaki, Hanae (2000), '1998 Excavations at Jazirat al-Hulayla.' *Bulletin of Archaeology, The University of Kanazawa* 25: 118–69. [In Japanese.]

Sasaki, Tatsuo and Sasaki, Hanae (2011), 'Excavations at Al-Ali Islamic Site.' *Bulletin of Archaeology, The University of Kanazawa* 32: 18–46. [In Japanese.]

Schacht, Joseph (1964), *An Introduction to Islamic Law*. Oxford: Clarendon Press.

Schottenhammer, Angela (2016), 'China's Gate to the Indian Ocean: Iranian and Arab Long-Distance Traders.' *Harvard Journal of Asiatic Studies* 76 (1–2): 135–79.

Seligman, Jon and Zur, Shachar (2021), 'An Early Islamic Mosque and Farmhouse at Naḥal Peḥar (Rahat) and the Islamification of the Countryside.' In Amir Golani, Daniel Varga, Gunnar Lehmann and Yana Tchekhanovets (eds), *Archaeological Excavations and Research Studies in Southern Israel. Collected Papers (17th Annual Conference)*, pp. 25–40. Jerusalem: Israel Antiquities Authority.

Serjeant, Robert B. (1978), 'Historical Sketch of the Gulf in the Islamic Eras from the 7th to the 18th Century AD.' In Beatrice De Cardi (ed.), *Qatar Archaeological Report. Excavations 1973*, pp. 147–63. Oxford: Oxford University Press and Qatar National Museum.

Shanks, Michael (2007), 'Symmetrical Archaeology.' *World Archaeology* 39: 589–96.

Sijpesteijn, Petra (2007), 'New Rule over Old Structures: Egypt after the Muslim Conquest.' In Harriet Crawford (ed.), *Regime change in the Ancient Near East and Egypt, from Sargon of Agade to Saddam Hussein*, pp. 183–200. Proceedings of the British Academy 136. London: Oxford University Press and British Academy.

Silva Santa-Cruz, Noelia (2013), 'La mano de Fátima.' *Revista Digital de Iconografía Medieval*, Vol. V (10): 17–25.

Silverstein, Adam (2010), *Islamic History: A Very Short Introduction*. Oxford: Oxford University Press.

Simonet, Francisco Javier (1983 [1897]), *Historia de los Mozárabes de España, Vol. II: De Abderramán I a Mohamed I (años 756 a 870)*. Madrid: Ediciones Turner.

Slot, Ben J. (1993), *The Arabs of the Gulf 1602–1784*. Leidschendam: Self-published.

Stargardt, Janice (2014), 'Indian Ocean Trade in the Ninth and Tenth Centuries: Demand, Distance, and Profit.' *South Asian Studies* 30 (1): 35–55.

al-Ṭabarī [Abū Jaʿfar Muḥammad ibn Jarīr al-Ṭabarī] (1994), *The Conquest of Iran*, trans. Rex Smith, The History of al-Ṭabarī vol. XIV. Albany: State University of New York Press.

Terés, Elías (1957), 'Linajes árabes en al-Andalus según la Ŷamhara de Ibn Ḥazm.' *Al-Andalus* XXII: 53–376.

Thorold, Alan (1987), 'Yao Conversion to Islam.' *Cambridge Anthropology* 12 (2): 18–28.

Tikhonov, Igor (2007), 'Archaeology at St Petersburg University (from 1724 until today).' *Antiquity* 81: 446–56.

Tomber, Roberta (2008), *Indo-Roman Trade. From Pots to Pepper*. London: Duckworth.

Trigger, Bruce (2006), *A History of Archaeological Thought*. Cambridge: Cambridge University Press.

Trimingham, J. Spencer (1968), *The Influence of Islam in Africa*. London: Longman.

Varisco, Daniel (2005), *Islam Obscured: The Rhetoric of Anthropological Representation*. Palgrave: New York.

Velázquez Bosco, Ricardo (1912), *Arte del Califato de Córdoba. Medina Azzahra y Alamiriya*. Madrid: Junta para Ampliación de Estudios e Investigaciones Científicas.

Velázquez Bosco, Ricardo (1922–23), *Excavaciones en Medina Azahara. Memoria sobre Lo Descubierto en Dichas Excavaciones*. Madrid: Junta Superior de Excavaciones y Antigüedades.

Vernet, Juan (1999), *Lo que Europa Debe al Islam de España*. Barcelona: El Acantilado.

Vernoit, Stephen (1997), 'The Rise of Islamic Archaeology.' *Muqarnas: An Annual of the Visual Cultures of the Islamic World* 14: 1–10.

Vickers, Miranda (2002), *The Cham Issue. Albanian National and Property Claims in Greece*. Royal Military Academy Sandhurst: The Conflict Studies Research Centre.

Vickers, Miranda (2007), *The Cham Issue: Where to Now?* Defence Academy of the United Kingdom: The Conflict Studies Research Centre.

Walker, Bethany, Insoll, Timothy and Fenwick, Corisande (2020a), 'Editors' introduction.' In Bethany Walker, Timothy Insoll and Corisande Fenwick (eds), *The Oxford Handbook of Islamic Archaeology*, pp. 1–16. Oxford: Oxford University Press.

Walker, Bethany, Insoll, Timothy and Fenwick, Corisande (eds) (2020b), *The Oxford Handbook of Islamic Archaeology*. Oxford: Oxford University Press.

Walmsley, Alan (2000), 'Production, Exchange and Regional Trade in the Islamic East Mediterranean: Old Structures, New Systems?' In Inge Lyse Hansen and Chris Wickham (eds), *The Long Eighth Century. Production, Distribution and Demand*, pp. 265–343. Leiden: Brill.

Walmsley, Alan (2007), *Early Islamic Syria: An Archaeological Assessment*. London: Duckworth.

Walmsley, Alan and Damgaard, Kristoffer (2005), 'The Umayyad Congregational Mosque of Jarash in Jordan and its Relationship to Early Mosques.' *Antiquity* 79 (304): 362–78.

Watson, Oliver (2004), *Ceramics from Islamic Lands*. London: Thames and Hudson.

Wazir, Burhan (2017), 'Finsbury Park van attack: why an imam saved a terror suspect.' *The Guardian*, 19 December 2017. Available online: https://www.theguardian.com/news/2017/dec/19/finsbury-park-van-attack-why-imam-mohammed-mahmoud-saved-terror-suspect, visited on 22 August 2024.

Webmore, Timothy (2007), 'What About "One More Turn after the Social" in Archaeological Reasoning?' *World Archaeology* 39: 563–78.

Whitcomb, Donald (1986), *Before the Roses and Nightingales. Excavations at Qasr-I Abu Nasr, Old Shiraz*. New York: The Metropolitan Museum of Art.

Whitcomb, Donald (2009a), 'From Pastoral Peasantry to Tribal Urbanites: Arab Tribes and the Foundation of the Islamic State in Syria.' In Jeffrey Szuchman (ed.), *Nomads, Tribes and the State in the Ancient Near East. Cross-Disciplinary Perspectives*. Oriental Institute Seminars Vol 5, pp. 241–59. Chicago: The Oriental Institute of the University of Chicago.

Whitcomb, Donald (2009b), 'The Gulf in the Early Islamic Period: The Contribution of Archaeology to Regional History.' In Lawrence G. Potter (ed.), *The Persian Gulf in History*, pp. 71–87. New York: Palgrave Macmillan.

Whitehouse, David (2009), *Siraf: History, Topography and Environment*. Archaeological Monograph Series 1. Oxford: Oxbow Books and The British Institute of Persian Studies.

Wickham, Chris (1984), 'The Other Transition: From the Ancient World to Feudalism.' *Past Present* 103: 3–36.

Witmore, Christopher G. (2007), 'Symmetrical Archaeology: Excerpts of a Manifesto.' *World Archaeology* 39: 546–62.

Yoltar-Yildirim, Ayşin (2013), 'Raqqa: The Forgotten Excavation of an Islamic Site in Syria by the Ottoman Imperial Museum in the Early Twentieth Century.' *Muqarnas: An Annual of the Visual Cultures of the Islamic World* 30: 73–93.

Index

Abbasid 94, 117
Abbasid Caliphate 118–19
'Abd al-Mālik (Umayyad Caliph) 60
'Abd al-Raḥmān I al-Dākhil (Umayyad emir of Cordoba) 75
Abla (in al-Andalus) 61–2
al-Ablī (Andalusi warrior and poet) 61–2
Abode of Islam, the (*dār al-Islām*) 4, 32
Abū Bakr 115
Abū-l-Baqī (name on a bowl of the David Collection) 73
Acién, Manuel 33–6, 38, 52, 94, 96–7, 100, 115, 134
act of identity in Marranci's work 50–1, 110
'actant' 71
action (in Asad's argument) 6–8, 10–11, 69, 133, 137
Actor-Network Theory 71
actual-virtual (in assemblage theory) 79, 81, 83–4, 86, 89, 101–2, 110, 131, 137–8
agency (in structuration theory) 11–12
Agra 25
Ahmed, Shahab 18–20, 45–6, 54, 62, 66, 69, 72–3, 90–1, 93, 112, 131, 135, 137, 139
  criticism to Islamicate concept 37–8, 134
  definition of Islam 16–17
  Islamic beings 55–7, 84–7
  meaning 15–16, 54, 56–8, 133–4, 140–1
  on one or many Islams 44
Albania 63–6, 84
Albanian Constitution of 1976 65

alcadafe (large container in the Vega of Granada) 106–11
Alevism 65
'Alī (the Prophet's son-in-law) 57, 60
Almeria 61, 99
Almohads 42, 95
Almoravid 95, 98, 131
almsgiving (Pillar of Islam) 60
al-Andalus 31, 33–6, 60–2, 94, 96–9, 107, 109, 113, 115, 119, 134
Anthropology and the Cognitive Challenge (book by Bloch) 52
Antigüedades Árabes de España (book of Islamic antiquities edited in Spain) 21
Anti-Oedipus (book by Deleuze and Guattari) 73, 76
Apostolos-Cappadona, Diane 60
Al-Aqṣā Mosque 73–5, 78–80, 83–4
Arabs 60–2, 113, 115, 119
Arabia 115, 121
Arabian Sea 24
Arabic language 28, 60–2, 64
Archaeology of Cosmos (book by Pauketat) 70
Archaeology of Islam (book by Insoll) 12, 22–3, 42
Aristotle 76
Asad, Talal 5–11, 13–14, 17–18, 38, 55
Asia 37
al-'Askar 117
assemblage (in assemblage theory) 77–91, 93, 101–3, 105, 109–13, 122, 125–6, 129–31, 135–6, 139, 141
Atatürk 75

autobiographical memories, *see* autobiographical self
autobiographical self 47–50, 52

Baghdad 117, 120
Bahrein 43, 115, 122
Balearic Islands 94
Balkans-to-Bengal cultural complex 16, 38, 139
Bangladesh 25
Barceló, Miquel 34, 36
Barrett, John 55
Basra 73, 117, 119, 121, 123
Ibn Baṭṭūṭah 25
becoming (in Deleuze's work) 102
becoming Islamic 57–8, 69, 100–2, 125–9, 137–9, 141
Being Islamic (short for the title of Ahmed's book), *see What is Islam? The Importance of Being Islamic* (book by Ahmed)
Bektashism 65
belief in Cantwell Smith's argument 5–8, 11, 14–15, 46, 69, 133, 137
see also faith in Cantwell Smith's argument
Bengal, East 24–6, 39–43, 134
Bennet, Jane 72
Berbers 32, 99
Bilād al-Qadīm, 122
'blob' (in Bloch's work) 52, 55
Bloch, Maurice 52, 54–6
Bourdieu, Pierre 11–12
bowl of the David Collection 73–8, 81–4, 89–90
Brahmanic civilization 26
Braudel, Ferdinand 12
British 114
Bulliet, Richard 29–33, 35–6, 38, 94, 134
bundle (in Pauketat's work) 70
Bushehr 122

Butrint 63
Byzantium 59

Cairo 117
Caliphate (Middle East) 113–16, 119
call for pray (*adhān*) 62, 64
Campiña of Jaen 104
campsite, nomadic 120–9
Çams 63–5
Cantwell Smith, Wilfred 3–8, 14–16, 18, 46, 55, 88
Capitalism and Schizophrenia, *see Anti-Oedipus* (book by Deleuze and Guattari) and *Thousand Plateaus, A* (book by Deleuze and Guattari)
de Cardi, Beatrice 122
Castile 75
Central Asia 21
chaîne operatoire 109–10
change (in neomaterialist archaeological theory) 88–90
Charles, King (V of Naples and Sicily and III of Spain) 21
China 58, 116–17, 119–20
China Sea 120
Christianity 8, 27, 38, 61, 124, 133
clash of civilizations 140
coalescence (technological and cultural) 108–11, 113–14, 130–1
Coast of Granada 104
coding (in assemblage theory) 80–1, 84, 89, 135, 139
conjuncture 12
Constantinople 59, 75
Constitution of Society (book by Giddens) 12
Con-Text 16, 18, 54, 56–9, 61–3, 65–7, 69–70, 72–3, 81, 83–9, 91, 93–4, 100–1, 108–9, 112–13, 130, 134–41

Index

in loco 57–9, 63, 65–6, 81, 101
in toto 57, 65
conversion, in Bulliet's work, *see* curve of conversion; in Eaton's work, *see* phases of conversion in Eaton's work
Conversion to Islam in the Medieval Period (book by Bulliet) 29
cooking pots in the Vega of Granada 102–6, 108–11, 113, 130
Copenhagen 73–4, 78, 83
Cordoba 61–3, 75–6, 94, 96, 100
Umayyad state 34–6, 94, 96–101, 108–9, 114
core consciousness, *see* core self
core self 48–9
Crellin, Rachel 73, 90, 135
Crescent and Star, the 59
Crowded Desert Project, the 122, 127
curve of conversion 29–33

Damascus, Umayyad Caliphate of 94
Damasio, Antonio 47–8
David Collection (in Copenhagen) 73–5, 77–8, 84
declaration of faith (Pillar of Islam) 60, 62
decoding (in assemblage theory), *see* coding (in assemblage theory)
Delanda, Manuel 72, 77, 82, 90
Deleuze, Giles 20, 72–3, 82–3, 85–6, 91, 93, 101, 109, 112, 131, 135, 138–9, 141
on being and emergence 76–9, 86–8
Delhi 25
deterritorialization (in assemblage theory), *see* territorialization (in assemblage theory)
Difference and Repetition (book by Deleuze) 72, 76

differenciation (in assemblage theory, *see* differentiation-differenciation (in assemblage theory)
differentiation-differenciation (in assemblage theory) 81–4, 86, 89, 91, 109–10, 131, 138
al-Dīn (the religión [Islam]) 4, 59
discursive tradition (Islamic) 10–11, 13–14, 17
dispersion (technological and cultural) 108–11, 113, 130–1
dolium (large container in the Vega of Granada) 106–7, 110
Dome of the Rock 60
Donner, Fred McGraw 7, 124
doxa 11, 46
Durkheim, Émile 9

East Africa 116
Eastern Arabia 115–16, 122, 129
Eaton, Richard 24–6, 39–44, 58, 90, 134
Encyclopaedia of Islam 2 3–7, 18, 28, 133
entanglement theory (in Hodder's work) 70–2
Egypt 21, 31, 94, 117–18
emotion in Damasio's and Marranci's works 47–51
Enlightenment 26
Erdoğan, Recep Tayyip 76
Ethiopia 43, 134
événement 12, 130
Evil Eye, the 60
Excellent City, The (al-Fārābī's work) 55–6
extended consciousness (in Damasio's work), *see* autobiographical self (in Damasio's and Marranci's works)

faith 13
  in Ahmed's work, 15
  in Cantwell Smith's work, *see*
    belief in Cantwell Smith's
    work
al-Fārābī 55–6
Fars 115
fasting (Pillar of Islam) 60
Fāṭima al-Zahrā' (the Prophet's
  daughter) 60
Fatima's Hand, *see* Khamsa
Fatimid 118
feeling in Marranci's work 43, 45–9,
  53, 66, 135
fiqh, *see* Islamic jurisprudence
Finsbury Park Mosque (London) 51
Fisher, Humphrey J. 42
Fitna, second fitna, in the Middle
  East 115
  wars in al-Andalus in ninth–tenth
  century 61–2
flat ontology 72, 77, 79, 85, 87
Fleisher, Jeffrey 80–1
fort (in Arabian archaeology) 118
Fowler, Chris 73
France 21, 94
Fusṭāṭ 117

Ganges 25
Gao 42–3
Gardet, Louis 3–6, 18
Geertz, Clifford 9, 49–50, 86
Gellner, Ernest 9
Genealogies of Religion (book by
  Asad) 8
Genil (river in Granada) 95
German Empire 21
Giddens, Anthony 12–13
Gjirokastër 64
Granada 60–2, 94–106, 108, 130
Great Britain 21
Greece 64–5
Guangzhou 119–20
Guattari, Félix 72–3, 79, 82–3, 135

Guichard, Pierre 33–5
Gulf, the 114–26, 129, 131
Gutiérrez Lloret, Sonia 35

habitus 11
Hadith 4, 10, 57, 137
haeccity 76–7, 111
Hagia Sophia in Istanbul 63, 75–6, 84
Hainan 120
Haram al-Sharīf (the 'Noble
  Sanctuary' in Jerusalem)
  73
Harar 43
hard lime-spalled wares (HARLIM,
  in the Gulf) 126
Harlaa 43
Harris, Oliver 73, 77, 82, 135
Herculaneum 21
hermeneutical engagement, *see*
  Ahmed, Shahab on
  hermeneutical engagement
Hijaz 123
Hinduism 25–6
Hodder, Ian 70–1
Hodgson, Marshall 36–8, 52, 94, 134,
  136
Holy Wisdom Church 75
Horn of Africa 43
Hoxha, Enver 65
Huan Ch'ao 119
humanness 27, 53–6
Huntingdon, Samuel 140

Iberia 21, 30–3, 35, 93, 95, 106
Iberian Peninsula 94–5, 113
Idea (in Deleuze's work) 81, 83
identity, in anthropology 47–52,
  66–7
  Islamic, *see* Islamic identity (and
    Con-Text) *and also* Islamic
    identity (in Marranci's
    work)
Ifrīqiyya 94
Ilbīra 61–2, 95, 97–9, 104, 108, 130

Index

Iliberis 95
īmān (maṣdar) 6-7
Immigration model in Eaton's work 24
India 24-5, 38, 116, 121, 123
Indian Ocean 93, 116, 119
individual (in anthropology), see identity (in anthropology)
Indonesia 9
Ingold, Tim 71-2
Insoll, Timothy
   definition of Islam 12-14, 18, 70
   Islamic archaeology 23
   Islamization as a process 58, 72, 90
   Islamization of Sub-Saharan Africa 41-4, 134
   Islamization of Bahrein 42
intensity (in assemblage theory) 79-81, 83, 126, 137
Iran 30-1, 115, 121-3, 126, 129
Iranian kingship 28
Iranian Plateau 24
Iraq 30-1, 73, 115, 117-18, 121-3, 125
islām (maṣdar) 3-4, 6-7, 59
Islam
   definition 1-20, 36, 39-40, 52-3, 66, 70, 88, 91, 133-4, 137
   entanglements and relationships 18-19
   and history 13-15, 17-18, 20, 27-8
   markers of 28, 62-3, 66, 136
   reification 3-6, 8
Islam Observed (book by Geertz) 9
Islamdom 37
Islamic
   anthropology 9-10, 13, 21-3, 26
   archaeology 2, 13, 19
   being (and correlates: person and thing) 15, 18-20, 45, 54-5, 69, 73, 83-9, 91, 93, 100-1, 112-13, 122, 125-6, 129-31, 134-5, 138, 141

Con-Textual assemblage 83-90, 93, 101, 103, 111-13, 129-31, 135-9, 141
identity
   and Con-Text 59-67
   in Marranci's work 19, 45-6, 50-3, 66, 135
jurisprudence (*fiqh*) 4, 38
philosophy 38
school (building) 41
social formation (Acién's theory) 33-6
theology (*kalām*) 38, 57
Truth and Meaning (in Ahmed's work) 56-7, 69, 71, 75, 134-5
Islamicate (culture) 36-8, 94, 134
Islamicate model of Islamization 94, 96, 100, 108, 118-19, 129, 136
Islamisation (book edited by Peacock) 28
Islamization
   as conversion 1, 21-9, 39. 134
   as cultural change 1, 21-3, 29-39, 134
   definition 1, 15, 19-20, 21-3, 32-3, 35-6, 38-44, 45, 58, 88-91, 93-102, 108-14, 118-19, 129-31, 134-41
Introduction to Islamic Archaeology, An (book by Milwright) 23
Istanbul 63, 75-6

Jaen 104
Javanese paganism 57
Jerusalem 60, 73, 83-4
Jervis, Ben 73, 82, 135
Jones, Andrew Meirion 73
Judaism 38
Justinian (Byzantine emperor) 75

Kadhima 121
Kehr, George 21

Kennet, Derek 122
Ibn Khaldūn 9
Khamsa 59–60
Khariji 115
Kirman 115
Kufa 117
Kush 122
Kuwait 120–1

Lands of Islam, the (*bilād al-Islām*) 4
large containers in the Vega of Granada 102–3, 106–11, 113, 130
Latour, Bruno 54–6, 70–1
lines of flight (in assemblage theory) 79–84, 89, 91, 102, 110–12, 126, 130–1, 135, 139
Loja 95
London 51
longue dureé 12
López Martínez de Marigorta, Eneko 36

madrasa 28
Maghrib 95
Mahmoud, Mohammed 51
Maimonides (Mūsā ibn Maymūn) 38
Mali 42
al-Manṣūr (Abbasid Caliph) 117
Manzano Moreno, Eduardo 35
markers of Islam, see Islam, markers of
Marranci, Gabriele 19, 45–56, 66, 86, 135
Marx, Karl 9
Mary, Virgin (Biblical character) 60
meaning 70, 80, 86, 110–13, 141
  in Islam, 15–16, 44–5, 56–9, 63, 69–70, 86–7, 91, 112–13, 125, 130, 137, 141
Mecca 79
Mediterranean 59, 99
meshwork in Ingold's theory 71

Mesopotamia 116
Middle East 21, 59–60, 64, 97, 120
Milwright, Marcus 23
miḥrāb 79–80
Milton, Kay 51
minaret 62, 64
miṣr 116–17, 119
monasteries (in the Gulf) 121, 124
Morisco 95
Morocco 9
mosque 18, 28, 39–40, 62–4, 73–6, 78–80, 83–4, 89–90, 124
Mosque of Cordoba 63, 75–6, 84
Mosque of Ilbīra 97
Mozarabs (Christians in al-Andalus) 61
Mughals 16, 39–41, 140
Muḥammad, Prophet 4, 15, 17, 24, 54, 60, 69, 114–15, 124, 137
mu'min (active participle of *a'manu*) 7, 124
Muqaddimah (work by Ibn Khaldūn)
Murwab 118, 120, 124
Mūsā ibn Maymūn, see Maimonides (Mūsā ibn Maymūn)
Musandam Peninsula 122
muslim (active participle of *aslāmu*) 7, 124
Muslim Society (book by Gellner) 9

Nasrids 60, 95
Native American cosmology 70
new materialism 20, 71–2, 91
Niebuhr, Carsten 21
nomadic semipermanent village, see campsite, nomadic
nomadism–sedentism (in the Middle East) 118, 120–9, 131
North Africa 12, 26, 60, 94, 97, 106

Oman 115, 117, 122–3
Omani Peninsula 116
ontological turn in anthropology 71, 85

Opaque White Glaze (ceramic type of the Samarra Horizon) 78
Orientalism 21–2, 25, 87, 140
Orthodox (Christians in Albania) 64
orthodoxy 9–11, 13–14, 16–17, 46, 69, 133, 137, 141
Ottomans 16, 21, 59, 75, 114, 140

Palaeospitia (in Butrint) 64
panera (large container in the Vega of Granada) 106–8, 110
Parangoni, Ilir 64
Pauketat, Timothy 70
Peacock, Andrew 28–9
Persia 21
Persian Gulf 42, 136
    see also Gulf, the
Persians 16, 120
phase transition (in DeLanda's work) 90
phases of Islamization 58–9, 90, 134–5
    in Eaton's work 39–40, 42
    in Insoll's work, *see* Insoll, Timothy on Islamization as a process *and* on Islamization of Sub-Saharan Africa
phases of transformation of the Vega of Granada 97–8
Philiates 65
pilgrimage (Pillar of Islam) 60
Pillars of Islam 60
postanthropocentrism 55
posthumanism 17, 20, 55, 87, 91
practice (in Asad's argument), *see* action (in Asad's argument)
practice theory 11–12
prayer (Pillar of Islam) 60, 62, 64, 80
Pre-Text 16, 54, 57, 66, 69, 134, 137, 140
Priestman, Seth 122
'proto-self' 47–8
Punjab 25–6

al-Qāhirah 117
Qarmatians 118
al-Qaṭāʿi 117
Qatar 93, 114–15, 118, 120–4, 126, 136
Qaṭarī ibn al-Fujāʾa 115, 129
qibla 62, 79
Quakerism 38
quiddity, *see* haeccity
Quran 3–4, 6–7, 10, 18, 41, 57, 60, 62, 137

Rachel (Biblical character) 60
Raqqa 117
Red Sea 118
relationality 71–2
religion
    reification of 5–6, 8, 16
    Victorian concept 8, 13, 17, 55, 133
Religion of the Social Liberation model 25–6
Religion of the Sword model 24–5
reterritorialization (in assemblage theory), *see* territorialization (in assemblage theory)
Revelation (in Ahmed's work) 15–17, 54–7, 69, 83, 114, 134
Riddah Wars (Apostasy Wars) 115
Russia 21

S-curve in Bulliet's work, *see* curve of conversion
Safavids 140
Sahel 43
Said, Edward 87
St Nicholas Church (in Butrint) 65–6
Samarra 117
Sassanians 115
scale (in assemblage theory) 88–90, 101–2, 112, 130–1, 139
schismogenesis 49–51

sedentism (in the Middle East), *see* nomadism–sedentism (in the Middle East)
shahāda (declaration of faith in Islam), *see* declaration of faith (Pillar of Islam)
shrine 39–40
Sierra Nevada (mountain range in Iberia) 95
Ṣīr Banī Yās 122
Siraf 120–2, 126
social Islamization (Acién's theory), *see* Islamic social formation (Acién's theory)
Sohar 117, 120–2
Spain 21, 35, 61, 63, 75, 136
stratum (in assemblage theory) 82–3, 89, 91, 93, 101, 109–13, 125, 130, 135–6, 139
structuration theory 12–13
Sub-Baetic System (mountain range in Iberia) 95
Sub-Saharan Africa 41–3, 93, 134
sūq 117
Swahili mosques 80–1
Symbol, in anthropology 49–50, 53–4
symmetrical archaeology 71
Syria 30–1, 119

Taifa 95
Tang 119
tautological circuit (in Marranci's work) 49–51
Temple knights 84
Temple Mount, the 73
territorialization (in assemblage theory) 79–82, 84, 89, 101, 110–12, 131, 135, 139
Text (in Ahmed's work) 16, 54, 57, 66, 69, 134, 137, 140
Al-Thānī 114
thisness, *see* haeccity
Thorold, Alan 42

Thousand Plateaus, A (book by Deleuze and Guattari) 73, 76, 82
Timbuktu 43
time (in assemblage theory) 88–90, 101–12
tinaja (large container in the Vega of Granada) 106–11
Torpedo jars 125, 127–8
transition (in Acién's work) 96–7
Tudmīr (East of Spain area) 35
Tunisia 31
Turkey 75
Turkish tribes 32
Turner, Victor 49–50
turquoise-glazed ceramics (in the Gulf) 123, 125, 128
Type A (cooking pot from the Vega of Granada) 104, 110
Type E (cooking pot from the Vega of Granada) 104, 110
Type I (cooking pot from the Vega of Granada) 104
Type M (cooking pot from the Vega of Granada) 104–5, 109–10
Type S (cooking pot from the Vega of Granada) 104–5, 109–10
Type V (cooking pot from the Vega of Granada) 104

Umayyads 61, 94, 97, 100, 113, 115, 122
of al-Andalus 34–6
umma 46, 50

Vega of Granada 94–106, 108–9, 111, 114, 130–1, 136
Venture of Islam (book by Hodgson) 36
virtual (in Deleuze and Guattari's works), *see* actual-virtual (in Deleuze and Guattari's works)

Vivari channel (in Butrint) 63
Vrina 63

Weber, Max 9
Western Africa, 42
What Is Islam? The Importance of Being Islamic (book by Ahmed) 15, 56, 66, 139
Wickham, Christopher 34–5

Xarrë 63–5, 84

Yangzhou 120
Yughbī 120–7, 129, 131

Zanj revolt 118
Zaropoula 64
Zirid 98–100, 130

www.ingramcontent.com/pod-product-compliance
Lightning Source LLC
Chambersburg PA
CBHW070338240426
43665CB00045B/2195